T0090313

WITNESSING POSTWAR EUROPE

The Personal History of an American Abroad

By Allan Mitchell

Order this book online at www.trafford.com
or email orders@trafford.com

Most Trafford titles are also available at major online book retailers.

Printed in the United States of America.

ISBN: 978-1-4269-4716-2 (sc)
ISBN: 978-1-4269-4717-9 (hc)
ISBN: 978-1-4269-4718-6 (e)

Library of Congress Control Number: 2010916669

Trafford rev. 12/09/2010

Trafford
PUBLISHING®   www.trafford.com

North America & international
toll-free: 1 888 232 4444 (USA & Canada)
phone: 250 383 6864 ♦ fax: 812 355 4082

CONTENTS

PREFACE

Traditionally, there have been two charges brought against the autobiographical mode of writing: narcissism and mendacity. In their self-evaluation, authors tend to glorify or at least to justify their role in the events of their time; and they frequently distort reality either by omitting untoward details or by embellishing them with fictional inventions. Although I cannot claim to have entirely avoided these twin pitfalls, this volume nevertheless represents an attempt to revisit the past with a proper concern for veracity and lucidity, just as any reader has reason to expect.

Many autobiographies have already been undertaken by professional historians to capture the circumstances of postwar Europe from an individual perspective. That list would include such notable personalities as Felix Gilbert, Fritz Stern, Peter Gay, Werner T. Angress, and Klemens von Klemperer – all of whom I came to know more or less well in the course of my career. They have shared one thing in common: they were immigrant scholars from Central Europe who came to the United States and became Americans before revisiting their native land after the Second World War. To be more precise, they were refugees from Nazism who wrote about how they fled their past existence and adopted another identity in the New World. My story is obviously quite different, in fact, the opposite. American born and bred, I found my identity transformed and molded by the discovery of Europe. That phenomenon was by no means unusual, since hundreds or thousands of Americans have had their lives changed by the experience of living abroad. To record my own case, then, may be primarily worthwhile not because it has been altogether exceptional but rather, in many regards, typical.

A number of friends have read various chapters of the following pages during the book's conception. All of them are mentioned below, and they know how grateful I am. Instead of including a redundant list, therefore, I merely want here to dedicate this text to my four grandchildren – Alena, Erica, Julian, and Melanie – for whom it was written.

Chapter One

THE CALVINIST

Europe became a serious part of my life quite by accident. So far as can be established, there is not a trace of French or German blood in my ancestry. My only real source for that conclusion is my mother's memory, still intact as she entered her mid-nineties, according to which my forebears could be identified back two or three generations on both sides of my family. All of them were Scots. She herself was born in a village near Glasgow and emigrated to America as a child. In my schooldays I proudly told my classmates how my parents had reverently stood on the deck of their ships as they passed by the Statue of Liberty. Only many years later did my mother confess that she and her two sisters had actually been fast asleep in their cabin as the vessel entered New York harbor. As for my father, he was like Andrew Carnegie born in Dunfermline, across the Firth of Forth north of Edinburgh; and like Andrew Carnegie he came to the United States as a poor young lad. Unfortunately the similarity ended there. Fame and fortune in the new homeland escaped him, as they did so many other immigrants in the first generation or two for whom America became the land of choice at the outset of the twentieth century.

Both of my grandfathers were artisans. One, who died before I was born, was an electrician who had worked in the Scottish coalmines caring for the lighting and the lifts. The other, my dad's father whom I knew well as a child, was trained as a mason, that is, a bricklayer. Apparently his prospects in the Old World were bleak, since he left Scotland to spend a year in South Africa before deciding that the racial circumstances there were unsuitable for him to settle with a family. He therefore returned and then departed once more for Pittsburgh, where the Scottish colony of which Andrew Carnegie was the star was beckoning for skilled labor. There, after moving his large family to the USA, he became what was known in those days as a "contractor," one who obtained and executed bids to construct houses and apartment buildings. My father, who was apprenticed as a carpenter and cabinet-maker, then joined the family building firm as a junior partner. Before the beginning of the Second World War they apparently did rather well as tradesmen in Pittsburgh. My grandfather lived in a large three-story brick house in suburban Swissvale; and my father and mother, with their two sons, occupied a more modest dwelling in Wilkensburg, likewise a contiguous part of the Smokey City. In those days that metropolis was still a steel town, and my only recollection of the first four years of life there was returning home from the neighborhood streets with knees and hands grimy from the soot that covered everything in sight.

None of the foregoing, it is evident, had much to do with continental Europe. Except for one thing. As it happened, I was born in 1933 during the first hundred days of Franklin Delano Roosevelt – and of Adolf Hitler. Suppose that Germany had not started a war in 1939, or that America had not entered it. More than anyone could have imagined at that moment, those two totally different personalities were mightily to influence every child of my generation. Oblivious to that eventuality, I moved with my family before my fifth birthday to Ashland, Kentucky, a rather sleepy industrial town (notably thanks to Armco Steel) on the Ohio River, midway between Pittsburgh and Cincinnati. It was there that I spent the war years, far removed from the violence and cruelty that were meanwhile convulsing Europe. A distant conflict makes scant impression on a ten-year-old boy scarcely able to read. And there was, of course, no television. Such thorough innocence is confirmed by some random and very faint recollections that remain from the years before 1945.

One was the news of Pearl Harbor. On the evening of that chilly December Sunday in 1941 my family gathered at the home of my Danish-born uncle, George Johnson, to hear FDR speak on the radio. That day of infamy does indeed live on in the memory of many Americans of my age, comparable only to the startling report many years later that President John F. Kennedy had been assassinated. Less searing but still memorable was the day that Singapore fell to the Japanese. Lacking any real conception of the war in progress, I had nonetheless hung a world map on the wall of my bedroom and adopted the habit of sticking tiny flags on pins into it as the military events unfolded. Unspeakably sad it seemed when the British Union Jack had to be replaced by a miniature Rising Sun. Another poignant scene ensued when I first sat down at the bedside of a young man, a neighbor scarcely ten years older than I, who had joined the army and was promptly sent to the Pacific theater where he was badly wounded. He had one leg amputated. Only a few months earlier he had been tossing a football to me as we scampered around a nearby cow pasture. There was an unforgettable shock in the realization that he was now crippled and helpless, that he would never play football again, my only small dose of reality from an imponderable conflict far away.

Once more, Europe played little or no part in those matters. Two impressions of that war front remain, one of them altogether ridiculous. During the war years it was impossible for radio-listeners to avoid the awful music of Spike Jones, leader of a popular band (invariably called "zany") whose hits were played over and over. The most popular of these was entitled "Right in the Führer's Face," which my playmates and I at our tender age found excruciatingly farcical. Naturally we had no notion of the literal meaning of the word Führer, not to mention the use of an umlaut, but the hilarious putdown of Hitler was obvious. That he deserved to be treated with more earnestness apparently did not occur to us. Then there was the celebration of VE Day in 1945, a wild melee in downtown Ashland that must have taken place in countless thousands of cities throughout the United States. I had never seen so many people at once on the sidewalks and streets, certainly not in such a state of ecstasy, while horns and radios blared incessantly in the background. In different parts of Europe the joy was doubtless no less riotous, but it must have been tinged with a deep sense of tragedy and the stench of death, from which we Americans had been blessedly spared. Only much later would the dark side of what had occurred in the early 1940s penetrate my benighted understanding.

Apart from those sparse and confused shards of childhood, one other may be recalled as a kind of confession. It requires a return to that cow pasture, located barely a five-minute walk from our house in Ashland. During the daytime a few cows actually grazed there, so that when playing baseball one had to be careful about sliding into what was assumed to be second base. The sandlot game of baseball ordinarily required that one player be selected as the plate umpire, and nearly always I was the person chosen. Why? One reason surely was that I was often positioned at shortstop and was thus well placed to observe all of the infield action. But

3

there was something else. My peers instinctively knew something about me for which none of us had a name. I was a Calvinist. That meant, in practice, that they trusted me to call out one of my own teammates if he should be tagged before reaching home plate. Europeans may not follow this terminology, but they will understand both the blessing and the curse of a Scottish Calvinism that demands earnest forthrightness with exacting honesty. Even as my religious faith began to wane (about which later), the deep mark of my rigorous Scottish upbringing became all the more evident. To be left with such an unbending – not to say rigid – character is not a matter for praise or blame. It is merely an inherited trait of life with which the self and others must come to terms.

It appeared altogether appropriate that I matriculated to Davidson College, then a small but distinguished Presbyterian men's school, founded in 1837 by the Scots, a sort of glorified monastery in the hills of North Carolina, north of Charlotte. There, at what was always referred to as "a liberal arts college," my introduction to Europe began. Yet it came in a thoroughly abstract fashion through the study of Greek, Latin, ancient and medieval history, and philosophy. To my knowledge, not a single European student was a member of the Davidson student body, which was composed almost entirely of well-to-do sons of professional families (doctors, lawyers, ministers) in the Carolinas. In that regard, as the offspring of immigrant artisans, I was somewhat exceptional. But who was to care about that?

Nowhere on the planet is there anything like the American college system, the jewel in our at times tarnished national crown. Certainly our high schools are generally inferior to their European counterparts: the lycée, the Gymnasium, the lärverk, etc. But the four-year undergraduate college often makes up for that deficiency. In my unexceptional case, it was a splendid opportunity to learn for which occupation I had some aptitude and for which not. One example of each should suffice.

In my sophomore year at Davidson my roommate was a bright fellow from Mobile, Alabama, by the name of Bill Dobbins. The son of a prominent physician, Bill was entirely dedicated to following in the footsteps of his father and had already declared himself to be a pre-med major. A medical career seemed distinctly possible for me as well, and so with some enthusiasm I enrolled with Bill in a biology course. In the classroom, when it came to memorizing bones of the body and the like, he and I did equally well, regularly receiving an A on our test scores. But the weekly laboratory was my undoing. Our teacher, Professor Puckett, gave us fetal pigs to dissect. To the manor born, as if he had spent his youth observing his father's technique, Bill carefully set about to pull back the outer layers of his specimen and pin everything so neatly that the inner organs could be exposed and catalogued. An exemplary operation. Au contraire, within two lab sessions I managed only to mangle and mutilate my poor little creature to such an extent that my fellow students were crippled with laughter at the sight. Professor Puckett began to bring visitors around to catch a glimpse of the ghastly scene in his laboratory. So much for my medical career. What patients would volunteer their tender flesh to the fearful thrust of my scalpel?

On the other hand, I was completely fascinated by and reasonably competent in classes of language, history, and philosophy. Most of these courses, as mentioned, were classical in nature and rarely touched on any subject beyond the eighteenth century. Probably most significant, as it turned out, was the exposure to biblical studies along with medieval and early modern philosophy. Outstanding for me was the Scottish historian and philosopher David Hume. In retrospect he remains a mythical author incapable of writing a false sentence. And his reflections on natural history led me to question deeply the Calvinist faith that had been tucked into my crib. The problem simply was that Hume posed questions for which I could find no adequate answer from the Sunday pulpit or from Scripture. The discussion of such questions went on not only by day in the classroom but also evenings in the dormitories of Davidson. One issue was particularly troubling. How do we explain the death of a young girl who wanders onto a roadway and is struck by a passing truck? Can we really believe that God should be so heartless as to predestine this accident and that the girl was created solely to experience such an awful fate? Banal as this example may seem, it plagued my thoughts throughout the four years of college and gnawed away the contours of my Calvinist faith. But if not religion, then what? The response in a word was history. To understand ourselves and the world in which we live, I concluded, there is no more rewarding academic discipline, one that moreover does not posit predestination, "intelligent design," or an Unmoved Mover.

All very well, except that I knew so little of that world, isolated as I was on a tiny speck of Carolina earth where time seemed to stand still. As it happened, the way out – or, stated more heroically, the path to discovery – presented itself in a most unanticipated form. By the time of my senior year at Davidson I had decided to try my luck in graduate school at some university as preparation for the career of a professional historian. Accordingly, a host of applications had to be filled out in search of a fellowship, without which I would be unable to continue my studies. Nearly a dozen such applications seemed to do the trick, from which I received a total of ten grant offers. It was while contemplating these options, one day in downtown Davidson, that I stopped briefly in a coffee shop. There I encountered a young man, whom I scarcely knew, who had spent a year in France as a Fulbright scholar and who was now a junior member of the Davidson French Department. *Faute de mieux*, as he explained, he had been appointed as a one-man Fulbright committee on the campus, but he was dismayed at the lack of applications so far received. The deadline was fast approaching – only four or five days hence – so why did I not do him the favor of applying? I confessed that it had not really occurred to me to spend a year abroad before attending graduate school, but, come to think of it, why not? It was on these preposterously skimpy grounds that I hastened about to request letters of recommendation from my professors – all of whom had graciously written in my behalf for other grants and who therefore only needed to recycle their prose. The application was thus submitted just in time through the delighted French instructor.

There was another coincidental twist to the story. The congressional law concerning governmental scholarships stipulated that each of the (then) forty-eight American states should choose a pair of grantees. Good fortune decided that one of those two Fulbright awards for North Carolina would go to me. My application stated that I intended to pursue a study of the Protestant Reformation and that I hoped to do so at St. Andrews in Scotland, whence my family had migrated at the turn of the century. It was all quite plausible, yet the national Fulbright selection committee had something else in mind (as I did not). There were too many applicants for the British Isles, I was soon informed by an imposing official letter from Washington, D. C., and since I had studied German at Davidson – only during my senior year in preparation for graduate school – would it be possible for me to venture instead to Marburg, the earliest Protestant university in Germany? Fearing that I must either accept that offer or nothing, I agreed.

In the background one can distinctly hear the winds of destiny blowing in directions that I had in no way foreseen. They now took me to Middlebury College in Vermont, where I spent the following summer after graduation from Davidson. Whereas I had gained a primitive theoretical knowledge of German grammar during the past year, my speaking capability was decidedly limited. Middlebury (where I later earned an MA in German literature) offered an ideal circumstance for an eager neophyte preparing for a year abroad. However appalling my accent may have been, I was set to sail for Europe. Literally so, since regular jet air traffic across the Atlantic was not yet in service. Hence it was, in mid-September 1954, that I reached New York City on a bus and stepped onto an ocean liner headed for Germany. All appearances to the contrary, I must wonder after all whether my departure that day was not predestined.

Chapter Two

THE YEAR ABROAD

If the foregoing account illustrates anything, it is the largely fortuitous circumstance that landed me in the harbor of Bremerhaven on a sunny late-September morning in the mid-1950s. For the experience that was to transpire I was woefully ill prepared. In that regard I was all too typical of most postwar Americans – except presumably for a narrow swath of elites on the eastern seaboard – who had accepted the end of the Second World War as a definitive settlement of European affairs and turned their attention back to their own parochial interests. Yet we know that much had occurred during the immediate postwar decade that was to change the face of Europe and to determine America's relationship to the Old World. Of these matters and more I had much to learn.

How are we to characterize that initial decade after 1945 – the one, insofar as contemporary Europe was concerned, that I had largely missed? The first and most basic fact was the physical and psychological destruction left there by the war. My grasp of that fact came quickly. After our ship docked at Bremerhaven, the Fulbright contingent, not quite 200 students strong, was transferred to a waiting train. As it pulled out of the station, outside on the railway platform, a small oom-pah band struck up a chorus of *"Muss i denn, muss i denn, zum Städtele hinaus,"* a tune about as folksy as it gets. We headed southward up the Rhine to Bad Honnef, where we were scheduled to receive a fortnight of orientation. On the first Sunday, with new friends, I hopped another train that took us a few miles downstream to the great city of Cologne, or what was left of it. It lay in ruins. None of us had ever seen such a sight of devastation. Although much of the rubble had been removed or pushed aside by the famous *Trümmerfrauen* (female cleanup crews), hardly any standing buildings were to be seen along the streets leading from the utterly flattened main railway station. Instead, most people were living, shopping, or plying their trade in huts and cellars. The sight was surreal, something out of a weird science fiction film. An exception to the rule was the huge Gothic cathedral of Cologne, whose immense spires miraculously loomed above the shattered urban landscape. Even that edifice had not escaped significant damage. It was raining that day, and there were puddles here and there inside the nave where precipitation was leaking in through cracks in the roof. Canvas strips flapped in the wind where once stained-glass windows had stood. Without having witnessed the war, I arrived soon enough after its climax to perceive the terrible pounding that Germany had absorbed, an astonishing and indelible impression later reinforced by my visits to the inner cities of Hamburg, Berlin, Dresden, and Munich.

Parenthetically, although this gets ahead of my story, it is worthwhile to record the lasting conclusion I drew from this sobering experience. Little more than a year later I was finishing an MA degree at Duke University, where I submitted a thesis entitled "The Noble Brotherhood of Arms" (a quotation lifted from Winston Churchill), which treated the Allied wartime policy of unconditional surrender announced by Roosevelt at the Casablanca conference in January 1943. At Duke one of my professors was a political scientist named R. Taylor Cole, a member of my examining committee. During the war Cole had been stationed in Stockholm as a member of the OSS, the American counter-espionage section. There he became involved, as he disclosed to me, in secret negotiations in early 1944 with Heinrich Himmler. Apparently the possibility existed to swing a deal with Himmler for the SS to overthrow Hitler and to conclude a peace. Professor Cole was convinced that such an action, if successful as he hoped, would have stopped the war at least a year earlier than became the case and that it might have thereby saved the lives of millions of Germans in their battered cities, Jews being herded into extermination camps, and countless soldiers in the field. Understandable and humane as that may have seemed, it was not a viewpoint that I – belonging to a postwar generation – could adopt. Citing the unsettled conditions and stab-in-the-back legends that followed the First World War and that had led to Nazism in the first place, I argued that it was finally better to fight on to the bitter end, despite the dreadful cost, and to end German fascism once and for all.

Predictably, Professor Cole was displeased with my stubborn opinion, and the approach of my oral examination therefore caused me considerable trepidation. Fortunately, he chose in gentlemanly fashion not to dwell on our differences. I am aware that there is no golden scale on which to weigh such cosmic moral considerations. By the time I began to ponder them in the ruins of postwar Germany, they were in the past and could no longer be altered. Whatever might have been, the German nation that I found in 1954 was thoroughly humiliated, demolished, and divided.

That is to mention the second most salient condition of Germany after the war: its division into eastern and western portions (one hesitates to say states) as part of the Cold War, a development that had already become a fait accompli by 1954. The postwar political history of Germany has often been recounted and can in retrospect be rapidly summarized here. After the Yalta conference in February 1945 and the Potsdam conference in July and August of that year, the drift of German affairs was becoming clear. Germany's surrender to the Allies seamlessly led to the creation of three zones of occupation, soon to include a fourth when Britain and the US agreed to carve out an enclave for France in the southwestern corner. Nothing was more natural, whatever the agreements or disagreements of statesmen, than for the Soviet Union to claim the eastern third of German territory to be within its sphere of influence and then conveniently to redraw certain boundaries in Eastern Europe to serve its national interest. Exactly when to mark the beginning of the Cold War may be disputed, but Churchill's "Iron Curtain" speech in March 1946 was an unmistakable harbinger of it. It was followed by the creation of an Anglo-American bizonal commission in January 1947, the pronouncement of the Truman Doctrine of containment of Communism two months later, and the swift implementation of a West German currency reform in June 1948. Any lingering doubts about the implications of these arrangements were then erased by the Berlin blockade and the Allied airlift that lasted from late June 1948 until the middle of May 1949. The inexorable outcome was the installation of the Bonn Federal Republic (*Bundesrepublik*) and the German Democratic Republic, the latter better known to everyone on the street for the next half century by its German initials as the DDR (only a few scholars refer to the GDR). The seemingly immutable reality of a divided Germany, then, had been all but engraved in granite by the time I reached Europe.

Before leaving Bad Honnef, incidentally, I was afforded an opportunity to shake the hand of Konrad Adenauer. On a second rainy Sunday in the

Rhine Valley a selected group from the Fulbright contingent was told that the Chancellor would be emerging that morning from the small Catholic church near his home in Rhöndorf, only a few miles away, and that he wished to convey his best wishes to American exchange students. We arrived in time to see this tall, gaunt figure with a stone face ambling in our direction. He uttered a few pleasantries, hardly audible to me, and then insisted on greeting each of us in turn. Several months later, as I shall shortly explain, I also caught a glimpse of Walter Ulbricht, Adenauer's East German counterpart, under very different circumstances. Such chance encounters, of course, have little if any significance, except to afford a sense of time and place.

From Bad Honnef I left by train, heading up the Rhine to Freiburg im Breisgau, where I was to spend the next nine months at the university. Why Freiburg and not Marburg, as originally supposed? To answer that question requires a brief flashback to my trans-Atlantic crossing. Once aboard ship, as we pulled away from New York (when I did see the Statue of Liberty for the first time, though heading in the wrong direction), I set about to locate the fellow students with whom I would presumably spend the coming academic year in Marburg. Maybe they could individually forgive me for saying so, but they struck me as a rather uninspiring lot. In the meanwhile, I quickly fell into step with the gregarious Freiburg crowd, about a dozen lively and attractive fellow voyagers who had little trouble in persuading me to join them. What to do? Screwing up my courage, I passed one day from tourist to first class, where the director of the Fulbright Commission in Germany was comfortably ensconced, and I made my case to him for a transfer. Admittedly, the scholarly excuse was fairly thin. In the course of my college studies I had run across a one-volume history of the Protestant Reformation by a German professor, Gerhard Ritter, who – as I had somehow learned – was on the faculty at the University of Freiburg. Would it not be fitting if I would sit at the feet of this distinguished master? Perhaps I did not actually put the question in quite such a threadbare fashion, but rather to my surprise in any case the director agreed. For him it was a simple matter of striking my name from one list and adding it to another. But for me that single act was to have, in ways altogether unseen, elemental and enduring consequences. The comment is inescapable that this fateful extemporaneous decision was one more link in a long chain of coincidences that determined my European course.

The city of Freiburg had been almost totally obliterated in little more than twenty minutes one evening in 1944. The story was that an informal agreement had been reached to leave for the duration of the war both Strasbourg, across the Rhine, and Freiburg as open cities. But due to bad weather, apparently, an Allied bombing mission that had been scheduled to attack elsewhere inadvertently (?) dropped its payload of explosives on the lights of Freiburg. Again, as in Cologne, virtually the only edifice left standing in the city's center was the cathedral, which the famous Swiss historian of the Renaissance, Jacob Burckhardt, once praised as the most gorgeous structure in all of Christendom. Surely the gods smiled on the Freiburg *Münster* that night, and it remains as magnificent as ever. Consequently, despite the surrounding destruction, it was possible for townspeople to continue the tradition of holding a kind of farmer's market every Saturday morning on the cobblestone area around the cathedral. My fondest memory of student life there is munching a Bratwurst on that square on the weekend and watching the crowds milling about.

Yet who was in those crowds? That apparently harmless question need only be somewhat rephrased to pose – unavoidably – the most obvious and disturbing issue that a stranger from a foreign land had to face in Germany less than a decade after the fall of the Third Reich. Who among them had been a real Nazi, and who not? Use of the term "real" as a qualifier is mandatory, because the simple fact that someone had been a member of the Party was manifestly not a sufficient criterion – as American officials in their zone of occupation would amply learn to their consternation when they attempted to have every German adult fill out a questionnaire (*Fragebogen*) about their affiliations and activities after 1933. The results were chaotic and generally worthless. To give some idea of the actual complexity, it may be useful to offer specific albeit random examples of my earliest acquaintances in Freiburg.

The first was a young man called Fritz, in his late twenties, whose family lived in a downtown apartment overlooking the Dreisam River and owned a tiny hardware store (now disappeared) nearby in the main street. Like most able-bodied German males of his age, Fritz had been conscripted into the German army and, as a foot soldier, had fought against the Americans in France. Had I been only a few years older, he and I might have been trying to kill each other in 1944. But now, during my initial days in Freiburg, I was sleeping on a couch in his bedroom. There in the evenings we talked incessantly, attempting to sort out our similarities and differences. The fact that he had served the Nazi regime seemed utterly insignificant in all of that, and it is hard to believe that anyone could have conceived of Fritz as a criminal – certainly not I.

Before long I moved into my own tiny apartment, further upstream on the Dreisam, in the Sandfangweg, a pleasant lane in an undestroyed peripheral neighborhood of the city. From my corner window I could see across the river a small bridge that led right up into the Black Forest, an idyllic setting. My landlady was a war widow and thus representative of hundreds of thousands of German women beyond the age of forty. Understandably, with her husband a military man, she had been quite patriotic during the wartime and was likely a Nazi Party member or at least a sympathizer. She still had a copy of *Mein Kampf* (officially awarded to all newly wed German couples after 1933) inconspicuously shelved with several dozen other books in her little library. By nature she proved to be a generous and scrupulously honest person, one with whom I could find no fault. For her the past was past, and good riddance. For a foreign student like me, attempting to integrate himself and to establish good personal relations, that was fair enough. Indeed, it was the reason I was there: not to forget the bygones of Nazi Germany but to encourage the restoration of cordial relations.

This normal if naïve attitude was more problematic in the case of another young man, a tow-headed blond with striking blue eyes, who lived in the same apartment building. The physical image of an ideal Teutonic type, he was a devoted hiker and insisted that I occasionally accompany him on his daily *Spaziergang* in the adjacent forest, while he loudly declaimed that it was "*gesund, gesund.*" My own enthusiasm was rather more faint, as I was more used to bike-riding or roller-skating on streets. But when in Freiburg.... Besides, the problem was elsewhere. It was conspicuous that this fellow loved to make a spectacle of our acquaintance, invariably introducing me to others as "my friend, the American," as if he felt a need thereby to display his bona fides as a good German. It was all too reminiscent of certain southerners I had known in Kentucky and North Carolina who dilated on their favorite "negro": they just loved Sidney Poitier (his films, that is) and wasn't Marion Anderson a wonderful singer? Such professed adoration at a safe distance can only betray or create an uneasiness likely born of a bad conscience. A close friendship did not develop.

One final example must suffice. The first student at the university with whom I formed a close and lasting relationship (in 2004 he and I returned together to Freiburg to celebrate the fiftieth anniversary of our meeting there) was named Hans-Christoph Bömers, always simply HC to his friends. The grandson of a Bremen senator, he represented a wealthy

Hansiatic family and had a big personality to match. Being about my age, HC had only youthful recollections of the Nazi era in which he was in no way implicated – except through his family, a matter of considerable historical interest. His father Heinz was namely one of Germany's leading wine merchants, owner and CEO of Reidemeister & Ulrichs, a Bremen firm whose specialty between the wars had become the importation of French wines. Long an opponent of the Nazi Party, he was nonetheless obliged to join it in order to protect his business and his family. Thereupon he was appointed by the regime to the post of German *Weinführer* in the Bordeaux region, put in charge of bulk purchasing and distribution. His relations with the Party, however, did not improve (Note: years later, while researching other matters, I happened upon documentary evidence of a severe scolding for non-compliance that Heinz Bömers received from the German military administration in Paris). Particularly troublesome, he was at constant odds with Hermann Göring, who among others urged that Bordeaux's finest wines be exported to Germany at cut-rate prices and that the French vintners who balked at these measures should be dispossessed. To cut to the chase, one may say that it was *Weinführer* Bömers who prevented the seizure of such fabled wineries as Chateau Mouton-Rothschild and Chateau Lafitte-Rothschild, as well as blocking the confiscation of entire stocks of *grand cru* wine that would otherwise have been shipped for a song to the Reich.

Granted, these selected individual cases fall far short of a scientific survey. Yet taken together as the residue of one student's limited experience, they demonstrate at the least how difficult it was – and is – to establish hard and fast measurements to distinguish the guilty from the innocent. Little wonder, then, that Allied attempts to enforce a policy of denazification bogged down in a swamp of obfuscation, evasion, and confusion.

My own perspective during that first year abroad was from the French zone of occupation. The presence of a French military force, headquartered in Baden Baden, was not especially evident in Freiburg. Daily life at the university and in the town went on, as we now know, at a time that marked the beginning of a remarkable economic recovery, the so-called *Wirtschaftswunder,* under the aegis of the current Minister of Economics (and future Chancellor) Ludwig Ehrhard. Such improvement became apparent in small and at times almost comical ways. The restaurants and pubs began to fill up in the evening, when quantities of that delicious local white wine from the Kaiserstuhl were consumed. Chicken, which had been virtually the most expensive item on the menu in the immediate postwar years, was starting to become more plentiful and cheaper, notably in a ubiquitous chain of eateries called Wiener Wald. Perhaps the most striking of all in this regard was the revival of the venerable German tradition of an afternoon indulgence in Kaffee-und-Kuchen. With astonishment, over a Spartan espresso, I watched two portly ladies in a café each put away two gigantic portions of Schwarzwälder Kirschtorte (plenty of chocolate, whipped cream, and cherries), as if they needed to make a statement that the days of deprivation were over. The streets outside were still filled with bicycles and mopeds, although the appearance of autos, usually Volkswagens, was becoming noticeably more frequent. Thanks to my father, I was in November 1954 able to purchase a shiny new motor scooter that carried me on my first trip to Paris with a fellow Fulbright student, George Beech (later an outstanding medievalist). We stayed in the Latin Quarter at a little hotel, now modernized and much more expensive, on a corner right across the street from the main entrance to the Sorbonne. At the time I had no inkling that Paris would become by far the large city best known to me.

At the university I made an effort to integrate myself. I joined a student Bach choir that was preparing his Christmas Oratorio for concert. As a boy I had regularly sung in a Presbyterian church choir, but without nearly the same rigor and technical difficulty required for this group. After a few evenings of rehearsal I realized that a young German student was making a practice of sitting next to me and prompting me when I faltered. His name was quite ordinary, Werner Schulz, but his friendship became extraordinary after he invited me into his circle of comrades who frequently met at a nearby "milk bar." There I learned a lot about German student life, at least at that time. Unlike American teenagers who habitually pair off with a date, Freiburg students ordinarily gathered in groups of eight or ten without fixed relationships. No doubt some coupling was going on as well, but that was not evident within the clique. Nor was there a trace of drunken orgies. American-style milk shakes were much in vogue, whereas beer – to my surprise – played little or no part in the social proceedings of many university students. Among them everything had to be celebrated: the visit of a cousin, birthdays, an aunt's birthday, whatever. Only for *Fasching*, the moral equivalent of mardi gras, were such conventions suspended. Then inhibitions were dropped and in larger evening festivities there was wild dancing, necking, and considerable drinking, ordinarily in costume. My reaction to that phenomenon was

15

largely negative – or perhaps better said Calvinist – for it seemed that the excesses of the *Fasching* season represented a rather vulgar release from the somewhat repressed social behavior typical of the rest of the year. I must confess that my response to the Oktoberfest in Munich, even many years later, was much the same.

Meanwhile, on the academic side, I of course attended a multitude of lectures, *Vorlesungen* that always began promptly at fifteen minutes after the hour, and I also joined the seminar of the professor whose famous name had provided the opportunity to reside in Freiburg. The only catch was that Gerhard Ritter had years before abandoned his focus on the Reformation and returned to his true love: the Bismarck era and the First World War. Before 1940 he had labored extensively in Prussian military archives that were then destroyed by Allied bombers during the war. Hence he was one of the few scholars still possessing notes from all those lost documents, and on that basis he was beginning to write his three-volume magnum opus, *Staatskunst und Kriegshandwerk*, a massive history of German militarism. He also retained lecture outlines, sketched in the late 1930s, that dealt with Bismarckian diplomacy. These he presented now in the lecture hall, usually mumbling over his text – as the Germans say, *vor sich hin*, as if to himself – so that the only chance even for German students to catch a complete sentence was to sit in the front row or two. Occasionally Ritter would look up from this ritualized performance and declare impromptu why he no longer believed the version just expounded, offering instead to the now fully attentive assembly of a hundred or so students his more recent interpretation. Then it was back to mumbling. More edifying and comprehensible to me were the seminar sessions. Ritter had recently undertaken a research trip to the United States, and there at the National Archives in Washington, D. C., he had turned up a copy of the original Schlieffen Plan that shaped German military strategy before 1914. This theme was the subject of his seminar, conducted in a classical Rankean fashion with much attention to the analysis of documentary texts. I was deeply impressed by this exercise and by the bright fellow students who participated in it. All of which doubtless helps to explain why, again contrary to my original intentions, I became a historian of the nineteenth century and not the sixteenth. It also confirmed my notion that the most one can do in life is paddle one's little boat in an effort to remain upright in a rushing stream over which one has no control. Its banality notwithstanding, this was as much wisdom as I could muster.

It is well to record one other episode concerning Professor Ritter. Through his seminar I was acquainted with his chief assistant, Klaus Schwabe (who became much later a specialist in American history and a biographer of Woodrow Wilson at the University of Aachen). Klaus was the one who brought to Ritter's attention that a visiting American Fulbright scholar was attending his seminar, which resulted in an invitation to visit the great man at his home in the Mozartstrasse. Naturally I was petrified at the prospect but managed to appear promptly at his door for the appointment. It began with a gaffe. I was greeted by a maid, to whom I announced that I had come to call on "Dr. Ritter." During my college years all of my teachers were professors but not all of them had Ph.D.s – hence to call someone "Doctor" at Davidson was somehow a higher distinction than "Professor." Decidedly, such is not the case in Germany, where a doctorate was and is the most basic prerequisite for any university post, whereas the established full professor (*Ordinarius*) must always be addressed as "Professor Doktor." Well, that embarrassing matter once straightened out at the door, I was ushered into a large dark wood-paneled study with heavily laden bookcases from parquet floor to vaulted ceiling. After a formal handshake, also strict German protocol, Ritter sat in his big easy chair and I on a wooden straight chair across from him. Our conversation quickly became a monologue in which he described his Prussian upbringing and his longstanding disdain for the Nazis, whom he had always considered a bunch of lowbrow Bavarians. Like many well bred Prussians of his generation, including those military officers who had perpetrated the plot against Hitler's life in July 1944, it was precisely his inveterate conservatism that motivated his anti-fascist attitude. Ritter himself, despite his impeccable nationalist credentials, had accordingly been picked up very late in the war, after the plot's failure, and incarcerated. His story complete, the Professor excused himself to attend a meeting somewhere in the city, leaving me alone in his Wagnerian study to examine his library as the late afternoon sun streamed in through tall windows, partially hidden behind dark drapes. If this prose is overwrought, it should at least serve to suggest a striking memory. For a much more scholarly evaluation of Ritter, one should turn to the excellent biography of him written decades later by Klaus Schwabe.

The German academic year, unlike that of France or the United States, consists of a winter semester and a summer semester. In between, from late February to mid-April, students are free to roam. As I was splendidly equipped with a motor scooter and yearned for warmer weather, I set off with another German friend, Uli Fanger, on a two-month journey to southern France and Italy, my version of the historic Continental Tour. From Freiburg we crossed the Vosges Mountains through snow fields to Lyon, where Uli knew a family that provided lodgings. Then we headed down the Rhone, with me up front driving and Uli clinging behind, to Orange. It was while passing by Julius Caesar's gate at the entrance to that town and seeing this miniature Arch of Triumph from the first century B.C., that we began to discover not only Provence but also the incredible remains of the Roman Empire. The remarkably preserved ancient stone theater of Orange, where plays and operas are still performed, was most impressive. No less stunning was the Roman arena in Arles, les Antiques near St.-Rémy de Provence, and the amphitheater and the Maison Carrée in Nîmes. By far the most remarkable sight, however, whether viewed from below by the river or from atop the gleaming structure itself, was the grandiose Pont du Gard, a ponderous towering aqueduct testifying as no other monument in France to the marvels of Roman engineering. With our trusty green *Guide Michelin* in hand, of course, we moved on to take in other three-star sites such as les Baux, the castle at Tarascon, the walled crusader city of Aigues Mortes, and the charming village of Saintes-Maries-de-la-Mer in the swampy Camargue on the delta of the Rhone. Truly, as I was just beginning to learn, France is a beautiful and blessed country.

After such an exhilarating historical exploration, motoring along the Riviera seemed tame and somewhat anticlimactic. We scarcely paused to mingle with the tourists already flocking there to enjoy the balmy spring. Once in Italy we followed the Via Aurelia along the Ligurian coast to Genoa, near which I was much later to spend three pleasant months at a "think tank" in Bogliasco. It would be tedious to recite all of the stops on our month-long Italian tour, but a few stand out in memory. After the predictable tourist promenades in Pisa, Florence, and Siena, we were surprised by the ornate façade of the enormous cathedral in Orvieto, a town perhaps better known for its dry white wines. Just south of there we came upon the bizarre late Renaissance garden of Bomarzo, inexplicably awarded only one star by Michelin. Its grotesque statuary gives a unique and most amusing lesson in the art of decadence, and it remains in my mind as a fantastic place for visiting and revisiting.

Uli and I passed on rapidly through Rome, saving it for our return, and continued on to Naples. It was not the city but those famous surroundings that intrigued us, especially a side-trip to Capri. There we caught up with a mutual friend and fellow student from Freiburg, a lively girl named Monika Stolpe, whose father was a prestigious (Roman Catholic!) novelist in Sweden. Through her and that literary connection, my traveling companion and I spent a few nights sleeping on cots inside the museum of the Villa San Michele, famous for its founder, the late Swedish physician and author, Axel Munthe. Allow me to mention one touching moment of that stay. Walking alone in Anacapri one day, I happened to hear a refrain of "Danny Boy" playing on the radio from a neighboring garden, causing this homesick lad to shed a few tears. Presumably, Spike Jones would not have produced the same effect.

From Naples we took a ship, after leaving the motor scooter locked at a travel agency, and landed overnight on Stromboli, where we rented a room nearby the house in which Ingrid Bergman and Roberto Rosselini had inaugurated their romance, so we were boastfully told by some locals (Strombolians?) at a bar. More eventful was an attempt to climb toward the summit of the volcano, still visibly active, which had to be aborted because of flying hot ashes. Then it was on by boat to Sicily and ten days of hitchhiking from Messina to Palermo, and back through the hinterland to beautiful Taormina, perched above the sea. What sticks in mind, not surprisingly, are the stupendous Byzantine frescos of Monreale, for which Michelin should award at least five stars.

The return to Rome offered a chance to stroll and sample the city at leisure. Easily the most thrilling visit for me was the Vatican, where Michelangelo's *Pietà* (not yet behind glass) could not fail to astonish the beholder with its perfection. It was Easter Sunday 1955, and on that morning we headed to the huge colonnade plaza of St. Peter's cathedral where we were blessed, along with some 30,000 others, by Pope Pius XII. This pontiff's controversial past was at the time unknown to me, but I learned of it later in some detail from two different sources. One was Rolf Hochhut's challenging drama, *Der Stellvertreter*, which touched off a maelstrom of polemics both pro and con. Decidedly con, the second source was my colleague Guenter Lewy, with whom I shared adjacent offices one summer in the early 1960s at Smith College. We often exchanged chapters of our writing. He was finishing a study of the Catholic Church in Nazi Germany, while I was converting my doctoral dissertation into a book. Lewy saw Pius XII as a certified villain who raised no objection to the Holocaust and who deserved a vigorous condemnation, from which he did not shrink. In vain I suggested he might try to be more "balanced." As we can now see more clearly, he was quite right to reject that advice.   My own interest in the former Monsignor Pacelli was not the same, since my topic was (so the title of my first book) *Revolution in Bavaria*. In 1918 he had been the papal nuncio to Germany and was thus stationed in Munich since, appropriately, in the land of Bismarck's notorious *Kulturkampf* after 1870, there was no nunciature in Berlin. During the months following the end of the Wittelsbach dynasty, the Communist Party briefly took over the city in 1919 and actually flew red flags from the twin towers of the central Frauenkirche. It was my thesis in this study that Pacelli was traumatized by that experience and consequently became a rabid anti-Bolshevik, which helps to explain his comportment in regard to Germany and the Soviet Union after 1933. If so, those two conceptions, Lewy's and mine, were altogether compatible.

The rest of our trip may be quickly recounted: across the Apennines to Ravenna (more Byzantine frescos), Venice (what can one say?), and through the Brenner Pass (more snow) to Innsbruck. From there we descended to Lake Constance, crossed it with our scooter on a ferry, and finally regained Freiburg. There is no way that the previous two months could be adequately summed up, except to say that they were educational and unforgettable. Uli and I parted broke, bronzed, and infinitely satisfied. One further self-serving remark may be added. During the entire period, twenty-four hours a day it seemed, my travel partner and I spoke German. It was the best language training I ever had: hearing the same idioms spoken with the same intonation consecutively for many weeks. Henceforth my fluency in the German language – which is not to claim perfection – was a given part of my persona. What I could not guess was that it would eventually get me into trouble.

Less than a month later I was in Berlin. To explain how that came about, it is necessary to back up briefly to Christmas. As I was alone, living on a modest stipend, and yet eager to explore, I turned for advice to a student travel office at the university in Freiburg. They proposed an excursion by train to Vienna for the princely sum of 50 DM, about $12 at the time. So off I went, via Munich and Salzburg, and arrived in Vienna late one December afternoon. Tramping around the city with my suitcase, I found what appeared to be a decent and affordable hotel near the Ringstrasse. After checking in, on the way to my room, I noticed a sign: OFF LIMITS TO AMERICAN PERSONNEL. I had landed in a brothel. Still a virgin, I departed after a restless night of noises and giggles in the hallway outside my room. Fortunately I fell upon a student hostel where I inquired within. The guardian explained that all the student residents were away for the holidays, but he could provide a bunk in a dormitory on the fourth floor. Relieved, I moved in. Two days later another young man appeared. Arthur Satz was also a Fulbright scholar in Munich, a graduate student from Princeton where he was working on a doctoral dissertation about the operas of Berlioz (in Munich?). He had intended to go skiing in Garmisch that week, but the snow there was too sparse and he had decided instead to travel to Vienna to take in some operas. Like me, he had stumbled into the same hostel. We spent a week attending the Oper an der Wien every evening (the Staatsoper was still closed for repairs). Before parting, Arthur and I agreed to meet again in Berlin during the spring break. There all the American Fulbright students would be gathered and lectured about the superiority of capitalism over communism.

The Berlin that I first entered in late April 1955 was a city divided into four sectors of occupation, but this was five years before the erection of the Berlin Wall. Naturally we exchange students were housed in the American sector, meaning in my case a small hotel on the Kurfürstendamm just down the street from the jagged remnant of the Gedächtniskirche, which, given the amount of ambient wartime destruction remaining, did not seem especially conspicuous. The Fulbright gang was broken down into small groups, to each of which a German student guide was assigned. Of course, we all wanted to see East Berlin, particularly on May Day when there was to be a huge parade that would pass Unter den Linden to the Alexanderplatz and along the Karl Marx Allee. By taking back streets known to our guide, we had no difficulty in crossing over into the Russian sector and finding the parade route. The last time I could remember seeing a real parade was as a boy in Kentucky, when the marchers were mainly Boy Scout troops, high school marching bands, and squads of prancing majorettes. Thus the spectacle in Ashland was performed by relatively few while the majority of townsfolk watched. The communist notion of a parade was altogether different: most citizens should march, leaving relatively few onlookers. Since the street scene was thus literally a free-for-all, a few other students and I decided to join the parade. Who would notice? This animated fun lasted about twenty minutes until we realized that we were rapidly approaching the review stand in front of the red-brick Rathaus near the Alexanderplatz. There stood Walter Ulbricht and his fellow minions of the Communist Party and the Red Army, who were under strict police protection and the eye of surveillance cameras. We came close enough to catch sight of Ulbricht and the other officials, but discretion being in this instance clearly the better part of weakening valor, we dropped out to the sidelines. Just for the record, then, Ulbricht never received my enthusiastic salute that day, and my allegiance to unbridled capitalism never came into serious question.

Arthur Satz and I had arrived on separate trains from southern Germany, but we departed together from Berlin to Hanover. Our vague intention was to "do" Scandinavia. We therefore hitchhiked to Hamburg, where we stayed in a hotel just around the corner from the university guest house on the Rothenbaumchaussee (in which I was later to live for two years). We then took a train to Copenhagen, crossed by ferry to Malmö, and hitched another ride northward to Stockholm. With us we had two items. One was the key to an apartment that had been supplied by my Swedish friend Monika Stolpe (of Capri fame), whose father kept this residence in the city while he ordinarily resided elsewhere. The other was a phone number that Arthur had obtained from his (to me unknown) roommate in Munich. Once installed in the apartment, we therefore called the number and received an invitation to late afternoon Kaffee-und-Kuchen at a home on Bergsvägen in Lidingö, a northern island suburb of Stockholm. There we met the couple Walter and Ragnhild Hoffmann and their three exceedingly pretty daughters Ingrid, Gudrun, and Helga. To mention these names already discloses a basic fact about the family: they were German. During the war they had lived in Berlin-Wilmersdorf, where the girls were born. Walter Hoffmann was a chemical engineer by profession, with a doctorate from the Technische Hochschule in Karlsruhe, who spent much of the wartime at the Polesti oil fields in Romania. His wife meanwhile devoted her time to serving in the Red Cross, often greeting and caring for soldiers returning from the Russian front. She and her three Mädchen usually spent part of the summers near Malmö at the home of a Swedish grandmother. But one could not visit abroad for long periods under the Third Reich, and they regularly returned to Berlin – until 1944, when Allied bombing became intense, the Russians were approaching, and the war was almost certainly lost. They escaped to Sweden on a Red Cross boat commanded by Count Folke Bernadotte. Dr. Hoffmann then joined them after the war, learned Swedish, and found employment with a Swedish chemical firm in Stockholm. Hence the family and the house on Lidingö.

One instructive parenthetical comment may be permitted. Although Walter Hoffmann worked for the German government during the war, he was neither Prussian nor a Nazi. His own family background was divided between the Palatinate and Switzerland. Educated as he was, his profession led him to employment with the large industrial firm of Borsig in Berlin, whence he was assigned to Polesti to oversee the production of gasoline there. On furlough back in the German capital in 1943, he was one day walking in downtown Berlin when he came to a level railway crossing. The gates came down, and he stood with other pedestrians as a train approached and lurched to a halt. Suddenly he realized that human beings were huddled in the freight cars in front of him. He and the others froze, all of them knowing the truth. No one spoke a word. They may or may not have known that Berlin Jews were often assembled at Charlottenburg in the swank West End of the city and then transported across it to the East. In any event, the train shortly moved on, the gates were lifted, and the silent crowd dispersed. The details of this sobering scene, described to me about twenty years later during a long winter's walk in Sweden, rang true to the core. It captured better than anything I have learned from books the reality and the futility of daily life under a totalitarian regime.

Back to Bergsvägen, where the discussion flowed easily in German, with which all were familiar, along with occasional outbursts of Swedish, the adopted language of the Hoffmann girls. Like all educated Swedes, they were also proficient in English, unlike their parents. Avoiding any intimate details, let it simply be said that Ingrid and Gudrun offered to show their grateful visitors around Stockholm, and the ensuing week passed most agreeably. As it happened, Ingrid was soon to graduate from her high school and was scheduled to join her classmates on a group tour to Rome in the late spring. Conveniently, the Stockholm-Rome Express passed through Freiburg, where Ragnhild Hoffmann was born. On her way back from Rome, with the excuse of visiting relatives there, Ingrid left the train and joined me for a two-week tour on my sturdy motor scooter as another clinging passenger behind the delighted driver. The predictable consequence, which culminated in the little town of Langenargen on Lake Constance, may readily be guessed.

One other recollection of that trip comes vividly to mind. While circulating in the Black Forest, we stopped overnight in a village to visit an old family friend of the Hoffmanns. We found there an elderly widow, living alone, who ordinarily rented out a guest room in order to make ends meet. Staying in it at the time was a couple from Dresden. When they found out that I was an American, they immediately began to berate me about the horror committed by Allied bombers in the destruction of their city. To justify that merciless fire-bombing, there was nothing I could say. But the widow could. Behind her on the wall were photographs of her two sons in their German army uniforms, both of whom had fallen on the Russian front. She uttered a single sentence: "*Wenn Du sowas nicht erleben willst, sollst Du keinen Krieg anfangen*" (If you don't want something like that to happen, you should not start a war). The impact was devastating, and the subdued couple quickly retired for the night. Obviously enough, those words would not have had nearly the same effect had they been spoken by me.

The remainder of my academic year in Freiburg was an anticlimax, and I was ready to leave in the late summer. The return to New York would again be aboard a large steam vessel that I had to catch in Southampton. To reach it, as usual with my one small suitcase, I hitched across France with a French military officer of the occupation, who was going on leave to visit his family in Brittany. After an overnight drive, he dropped me off at the railway station in Caen, from which I might arrive by train at a ferry landing on the coast. For the previous nine months I had lived among Germans, who are for the most part a physically large folk. But suddenly, as I stood on the platform awaiting my coach, I became aware that I was the tallest person in the crowd. Bretons, one must suppose, are by nature a rather short race of Europeans. But that moment may also have served as a reminder that the Germans were not alone to suffer dietary deprivation during the early twentieth century. As for me, I was returning to a land of plenty after an experience that was bound to change the rest of my life. What if I had gone to St. Andrews?

Chapter Three

HARVARD

The late 1950s were an extraordinarily quiet time for America, at least insofar as foreign affairs were concerned. We were between the wars in Korea and Vietnam. And meanwhile Europe appeared to settle further into the confines of the Cold War. In 1955 West Germany officially became sovereign and was admitted to NATO. Also that year the Hallstein Doctrine proclaimed that the Bonn Republic would conduct no diplomatic relations with any country recognizing the DDR as a nation – the USSR curiously and significantly aside. This meant that "our" Germany had no formal contacts with any of the other states in Eastern Europe. In the year following, the European Economic Union was formed, and though Great Britain refused to join it, the "little Europe" of western nations was assured, along with West Germany's integration into it. The 1956 uprising in Hungary and its repression gave the Communist block even more of a bad name. In round and ominous numbers, between the end of the war and the year 1960, about three million persons left East Germany to try their luck in the West. Looking back, therefore, nothing seems more inevitable than the erection of the Berlin Wall in August 1961, whether one sees it as the natural culmination and ugly embodiment of the great European divide since Lenin founded the Soviet Union, since the collapse of Hitler's Third Reich, or since the onset of the Cold War. The steady bleeding of East German population, a flow always and only in one direction, had to be staunched if the DDR were to survive and a reasonable stability restored to Central Europe.

It seems slightly absurd to note that I completed my Ph.D. at Harvard only a few weeks before the construction of the Berlin Wall – two events of rather unequal import. After disembarking in New York in the late summer of 1955, I spent a studious and uneventful year at Duke University, but I decided not to stay there for my doctorate. My principal professor, a diminutive gentleman named E. (for Eber, a male swine in German, which caused him to wince when I mentioned it) Malcolm Carroll, was certainly competent enough, distinguished as he was as a Franco-German scholar and as an editor of captured German documents. Yet he represented a classical and dated form of diplomatic history, and he was near to retirement. Accordingly, I drifted instead to Stanford, as so often blissfully unaware of gathering circumstances beyond my purview that would determine my future course. Arriving one autumn afternoon in 1956 at an administrative building on the Palo Alto campus, I mounted a sunlit wooden staircase and knocked on the door of the chairman of the Department of History. It was opened by a tall slender man, aged about forty, with tousled chestnut hair and horn-rimmed glasses. He was Professor H. (for Henry, never used) Stuart Hughes, scion of a renowned New York family and grandson – as he always hated to have recalled aloud – of Charles Evans Hughes, once Chief Justice of the Supreme Court and the Republican candidate against Woodrow Wilson in the presidential election of 1916. By the time our conversation had ended, I was enrolled in his class of modern German history and his seminar on historiography. Unknown to me, he was writing his most famous book, *Consciousness and Society*, an intellectual history of European social thought between 1890 and 1930 (for which I later compiled the index). Moreover, Hughes had just received a call to join the faculty of Harvard University. It was, in other words, his last quarter at Stanford. Dumb luck, the rest followed. By the time that quarter was over, we had determined that I should join him at Harvard; or rather, that I should precede him, since he stayed on at a think tank near the Stanford campus to work on his book while I left in February 1957 for Cambridge, Mass. Once more, as two years before in Vienna, I tramped about in a strange snowbound city, with my still intact suitcase bearing all of my earthly belongings, looking for some lodging. On a tip from the University's housing office, I found a rooming house not far from the graduate center at Harkness Commons and forthwith plunged into another unpremeditated episode. At least it did not start in a brothel.

The first semester at Harvard proved to be dark and dangerous. I was admitted to the graduate seminar of Professor William L. Langer, then America's most acclaimed scholar of modern Europe. The class of twelve students met one evening a week at Langer's home on Berkeley Street in Cambridge, barely a five-minute walk from my rooming house. A regular procedure was rigorously imposed by Langer: one of the students reported on a research project for exactly an hour, followed by comments from the others and then concluded by Langer's own magisterial analysis that never failed to draw out the essentials and expose any weaknesses. Unfortunately, my report came very early in the semester, after only three weeks in Cambridge, that is, at a time when I could scarcely find my way to Widener Library. After struggling to spin out my thin research for a full hour on "The Pan-German League in Belgium before 1914," I was pummeled by my fellows, not unjustifiably. Then Langer spoke with his flat foghorn Boston accent: "Well, Mr. Mitchell, there seems to be something rotten in the state of Denmark." I felt a sharp pain in the solar plexus that paralyzed me with fear. Understandably, then, I worked fanatically without pause in the bowels of Widener for the next three months before submitting a final draft of my paper. It was well known that anything short of a grade of A from Langer might be the instant kiss of death for a budding career. Hence I was exceedingly apprehensive on the day I went to pick up my paper and giddy with relief to learn that I would not after all be bounced out of the Harvard graduate program. Postscript: no teacher more profoundly influenced me than Professor Langer, whom I came to know somewhat personally before his death. Besides, my apprenticeship with him brought an unexpected bonus years later in Hamburg when I became acquainted with Fritz Fischer, whose penetrating account of pre-1914 German imperialism, *Griff nach der Weltmacht*, kicked up a storm among historians of Europe in the 1960s – a vast topic seen by me through the tiny prism of the Pan-German League. There was, as Fischer was pleased to confirm, something rotten in the state of Belgium.

The next year was something of a blur or, as we used to say, a grind. My immediate task was to prepare four fields for the general oral Ph.D. examination, "the generals." One of them, incidentally, was the Reformation, to which I at last returned with a sense of irony after a long detour had led me off the course of Calvinism. After many months of silently camping out in my stall in Widener Library, with little respite from non-stop reading except to attend an occasional lecture, I stood for my exam in the spring of 1958 and passed it without any particular distinction. Meanwhile, I had applied for and received a generous grant from the French government – in reciprocity for the Fulbright program – to study for a year in Paris. Although I had acquired some training in

French at Davidson and Middlebury, my initial aptitude as speaker of a second European language was still deficient. But here was an opportunity not to be missed.

Crossing the Atlantic was once more by sea, this time on a French ship heading to Le Havre. Aboard I learned a valuable lesson in French etiquette: never say "*merci*" to a server who offers you a second helping at dinner. The food was delicious, and I would gladly have accepted another portion of, say, roasted duck. But our waiter would invariably turn away when I thanked him for the offer. In this instance *merci* means "no thanks." A simple "*oui*" does much better. Such an example may seem impossibly trivial, but my acquisition of colloquial French came in this manner, bit by bit over the years rather than in a swoop as had been the case with German. French has always struck me as more formulaic than the much more flexible and rich vocabulary of English. The common phrase "*il n'y a pas de quoi*," for instance, consists of seven different words that must be spoken rapidly and exactly in that order, not otherwise. It was regularly used by our French waiter aboard ship whenever I succeeded in thanking him for kindly steering a second portion of foie gras onto my plate.

My first residence in Paris was a small flat at 77 Rue Madame, quarters arranged for me by a fellow Harvard graduate student, Cecil Smith, who had previously lived at the same rooming house in Cambridge and who had just vacated the dwelling in Paris that now became mine. The apartment building, complete with a crusty old concièrge right out of Balzac, was located at a juncture with the Rue d'Assas, three minutes from the Jardin de Luxembourg, where I often went strolling or jogging. The proprietor was Monsieur Morin, an *inspecteur des finances* in the French Ministry of the Treasury. He had been an officer in the French zone of occupation in Germany for several years after the war, and we consequently had something in common to chat about.

A far more important address, however, was 27 Rue Saint-Guillaume, the seat of "Sciences Po" (formally, the Institut d'Études Politiques), where I took up a year of studies as an *auditeur libre*, something of an academic parasite, one not required to stand for final examinations. The list of faculty for 1958-1959 boasted the names of some of France's most illustrious intellectuals, such as Pierre Renouvin, Raymond Aron, François Goguel, and André Siegfried. But my attention was drawn to slightly lesser lights (who later became illustrious enough in their turn): Jean-Baptiste Duroselle (a diplomatic historian, eloquent, jolly, and rotund), Maurice Duverger (tall, slender, bow tie, fascinating on comparative political systems), René Rémond (best lecturer of the bunch, who held forth on political ideologies), and most significantly for me Alfred Grosser. My main undertaking for that year, apart from burrowing into the French way of life, was to define a topic for my doctoral dissertation. For that purpose, as it proved, the association with Grosser, France's leading expert on contemporary Germany, was ideal. Still a young man with a gorgeous trophy wife (his former student), the German-born Grosser created a lively enthusiasm in his seminar that was altogether irresistible. Rather like Gerhard Ritter in Freiburg, albeit with a totally different style, he was interested to have an American in his class, especially one who knew German. For those reasons his help was more than perfunctory, and it provided just the needed spark. By chance, he had recently accepted the assignment of reviewing a volume of Max Weber's writings and lectures about the time of the First World War, a period when Weber was residing in Munich. Grosser loaned me that book, wondering what I thought of it, and my perusal soon led me to a topic still largely untouched by historians: the revolution of 1918 in Bavaria. *Voilà*! But was it researchable? That question was promptly answered, thanks to Grosser's advice, by trekking over to the Bibliothèque de Documentation Internationale Contemporaine, then located in a plain brownstone building just off the Champs-Élysées (it is now at Nanterre near the Porte Maillot). There I discovered a remarkable collection of Bavarian newspapers from the period in question. Indeed, this cache of printed materials proved to be far more complete than anything that could be found in Munich, where Allied bombing had done extensive damage and created irreplaceable documentary lacunae. The outcome was that I spent more than half of my first year in Paris attending classes in the morning at Sciences Po and reading German newspapers in the afternoon at the BDIC. If that routine was not ideal for an immersion in *la vie parisienne*, it was certainly excellent training for a young scholar seeking a footing in Franco-German history. Moving on from Paris to Munich late that spring allowed me to plunge into archival material located there, so that the research for my doctoral dissertation was well launched before my return to Harvard in September 1959.

Mention of that date mandates a personal word of explanation. During my inaugural stint in Cambridge I had been joined by Ingrid Hoffmann, who arrived from Stockholm to take an administrative post at MIT. She lived on Beacon Hill in Boston, where we frequently camped out. Since I considered myself too young and unsettled to contemplate marriage at age

25, nothing was definitively decided before our mutual return to Europe. But in the course of my stay in Paris we reunited, celebrated an engagement in Munich with the senior Hoffmanns, and married on 1 September 1959 in a Swedish ceremony at the little church of Lidingö. These events, it is worth recalling, would not have occurred had I not four years earlier traded a Vienna brothel for a student hostel. Or, to repeat, if I had gone to St. Andrews rather than Freiburg. "I am the master of my fate, I am the captain of my soul." No more foolish words were ever written.

After sailing back to the United States on a Norwegian ship from Oslo, the newly weds settled down in a tiny apartment on Broadway in Cambridge, Mass. My second long sojourn at Harvard was decidedly more relaxed than the first. Appointed as a Teaching Fellow in the Department of History, I was assigned as a tutor in Quincy House where, not coincidentally, Stuart Hughes was a Senior Fellow. My chore now was to hand out grades, a far more pleasant task than to receive them. I conducted small colloquia to discuss problems of historiography, essentially a course in great history books, everything from Thucydides to Tocqueville. Meanwhile, of course, the dissertation had to be written and also, the summer following, to be further researched in Munich. During that stay in Europe, precisely on Midsummer's Night in 1960, our first daughter Catherine was born in Stockholm. The next academic year we lived in an apartment at Quincy House, which meant that she spent much of her first year of life in the courtyard there cooing and gurgling with admiring Harvard undergraduates.

My new exalted status included the dubious honor of attending Department meetings and faculty parties, a chance to meet and observe such luminaries as Professor Langer, Arthur Schlesinger, Jr., Oscar Handlin, "Bud" Bailyn (whose wife was Ingrid's colleague at MIT), and so on. Unavoidably, we also came into contact with the numerous celebrities who passed shorter or longer periods at Harvard. A few deserve mention. The charming Raymond Aron visited the campus to give a talk on the Algerian War, which he denounced; when loudly heckled from the audience, he was defended with vigor by Professor Langer. Willy Brandt likewise appeared, speaking halting but forceful English in a speech that foreshadowed his future foreign policy toward Eastern Europe. The playwright Edward Albee lived for a few weeks in Quincy House where, in the Senior Common Room, he seemed surprisingly interested in me. It turned out that he was writing *Who's Afraid of Virginia Woolf* and was doing some research on academics in search of a prototype for the character in his drama named Nick, a weakling professor (I trust Albee showed an equal curiosity about dozens of other young faculty members!). Another visitor for an extended period in Quincy House was George Kennan, who made a point of befriending resident faculty and inviting them to cocktail hours in his quarters. Attractive and honorable as he was, I could not forget an article that he had published – in the *Frankfurter Allgemeine Zeitung* or *Die Zeit?* – years before when I was a student in Freiburg. At that time, of course long before the Wall, he suggested the possibility that a neutral buffer zone might be created from Sweden to Switzerland, including all of the German territories, in order to separate (and presumably contain) the East from the West without the inherent dangers of close contact on fixed mutual borders. Now, at the beginning of the 1960s, he fully recognized that the time had passed when such a proposal made any sense.

By far the person who made the most impression was Henry Kissinger. Recently promoted to the rank of full professor in Harvard's Department of Political Science, he became a Senior Fellow at Quincy House and consequently appeared every Wednesday for lunch at the High Table (held literally on a slightly raised platform in the Quincy dining hall). I made a point of sitting near Kissinger, from whom a riveting monologue on foreign affairs might be expected at every gathering. He did not disappoint in that regard, dispensing inside information on all matters political during the period of John F. Kennedy's election to the presidency. Kissinger himself had obvious Republican leanings and ambitions, at that time attached to Nelson Rockefeller – and only later to Richard Nixon. As a rule, he took little note of very junior faculty persons and only once evinced much interest in my thoughts when I expressed my admiration for Adlai Stevenson. Kissinger scoffed at the notion that Stevenson would have made a suitable President, being much too tentative and indecisive. Certainly, as we later learned, the same could not be said of Nixon.

Much more significant than the celebrities or professors were my fellow graduate students at Harvard. They were the ones with whom we generally ate and caroused, swapped notes and ideas, discussed books and personalities, shared in joys and sorrows. In the course of my three and a half years in Cambridge I naturally encountered dozens of budding scholars, but, as is normal, only a few became close friends. If I mention here just four of them, it is necessary to omit others no less accomplished.

Among the drones specializing in the history of modern Germany, Barbara Miller Lane was the queen bee. Married to an engineering major at MIT, she regularly presided over a study group that met weekly at their apartment. Our relations were quite cordial, and once I even caught wind of a rumor that we had secretly become lovers. Sorry, that was simply not true, and I rushed to assure one and all that such was not the case, although I did on one occasion remark that I had always "hot thighly" of Barbara. That little Freudian slip also circulated thereupon and made my professions of innocence appear a bit lame. But innocent she and I were and remained. Barbara later became a professor at Bryn Mawr College and the author of an excellent study of *Architecture and Politics in Germany, 1918-1945*.

Fritz Ringer was German-born, and he still spoke with a noticeable accent despite a long and happy marriage to his beautiful American wife Mary. They had been college sweethearts when he attended Amherst and she Mt. Holyoke. The Ringers and the Mitchells often met in the evening for a bridge game or a community potluck. As he was very accomplished on the accordion, Fritz was frequently the life of the party, as he tended to be with or without musical accompaniment. His dissertation about German academic life before 1933, entitled *The Decline of the Mandarins*, was probably the best single volume to emerge from our coterie. Fritz taught at Indiana University and Boston University, where he directed a huge statistical study comparing France and Germany in modern times. Later, at the University of Pittsburgh, he returned to his first love, German intellectual history, and completed a work analyzing the writings of Max Weber. Alas, his health declined and he died prematurely of a liver ailment.

My closest friend at Harvard was Tom Skidmore, a sometime squash partner, who began in the field of German history – his dissertation was on Bismarck's successor as Chancellor, Leo von Caprivi – but who eventually became the most noted American Brazilianist of our generation. When a chair in Latin American studies fell vacant, the Harvard Department of History decided not to fill it but to tap several promising young scholars in other disciplines to divert their careers to that field. Tom was among those chosen, but only one was retained at Harvard: that was John Womack, whose brilliant book on Emiliano Zapata brought him instant recognition. Tom consequently left Cambridge to join the faculty at the University of Wisconsin and then Brown University. It is only fair to note that his scholarly output over the years far surpassed Womack's. It is also true to say that Tom had an unfair advantage to have the aid of his wife Felicity, daughter of an Oxford don and chief editorial assistant for Paul Samuelson at MIT. She was widely suspected of ghost-writing Samuelson's famous textbook on economics, but of course I would not want to encourage another vicious rumor with this hint. Stricken by Alzheimer's disease in his sixties, Tom nonetheless continued with remarkable courage to publish a revised edition of his authoritative *Brazil. Five Centuries of Change.*

For future reference, one further name must be added: Larry Joseph, who was a graduate student in the Department of French Literature. Our first meeting seemed incidental. At Quincy House I organized two language tables, French and German, which met for dinner once a week in a room off the main dining hall. Larry showed up one evening at the French table, and his skill with the language was immediately evident, so that I could not fail to take notice of him. But nothing further ensued at the time. A few years later, however, as I was leaving the Bibliothèque Nationale in Paris one evening, I spied this young man passing out the door and very originally asked: "Haven't we met somewhere before?" We had, and Larry soon became a regular dinner guest. As it happened, Smith College (where I had become a faculty member) had a vacancy in French literature, and I encouraged Larry to apply. Not surprisingly, he won the job and became for the next ten years a most compatible colleague (of which more later).

In June 1961, as noted, my apprenticeship as a scholar and teacher duly reached its end, and in my crimson robe I marched with hundreds of others in Harvard's annual academic procession to be hooded as a freshly baked Doctor of Philosophy. It was exactly seven years since my graduation from Davidson College and my first departure to Europe – seven years on the move that had, for better or worse, shaped my personality and determined the direction of my career. During all of this commotion my personal Europeanization was proceeding apace: European parents, European wedding, European studies and languages. In the meanwhile the line through the center of the European subcontinent was literally being set in concrete, and the Cold War had found a seemingly immutable form. The demographic fluidity and political uncertainty in Europe during the early years of my academic training were abruptly squelched by the erection of the Berlin Wall. Now John F. Kennedy and Nikita Khrushchev embodied the opposing sides in a duel that offered little apparent hope for resolution or compromise. Boundaries were drawn, questions answered, and lives shaped. Including my own.

Chapter Four

SMITH COLLEGE

Northampton MA 01060 is in many ways a typical New England town, except that there is no village green. And there is Smith. Politically as well as financially, Northampton is dominated by the College and by Roman Catholics. My European friends assume that America, or at least this northeastern part of it, is thoroughly Puritan and thus strictly Protestant at heart. But the reality is otherwise. For most of my decade there, the mayor was named Wally Pulchowski, who owned a little downtown drugstore that sold (so I was reliably informed) pornography under the counter. The majority of Northamptonians are of Irish or Italian extraction, but they stepped aside in the 1960s to give one of the Polish Catholic minority a turn in city hall as a reward for solidarity.

Where have all the Puritans gone? Many of them are to be found at Smith, whose straitlaced gentility and devotion to duty at a "teaching college" were still very much in fashion when the Mitchell family of three arrived there in 1961. Actually, three and a half, since we were pregnant with our second daughter Alexandra, born on a crisp January winter morning in Northampton's Cooley Dickinson Hospital – maybe not quite so romantic as Midsummer's Night in Stockholm but every bit as beautiful.

Allegedly we were to move right away into a new faculty apartment in the Fort Hill area, but the construction was tardy, the complex still uncompleted, and the need thereby created to find temporary quarters. We did so with an elderly widow in one of those large frame houses that line Elm Street, on which, five minutes away, the main gate of the campus stands. Since it was autumn, my walk to the classroom every morning was a glorious experience. Nowhere in the world, to my knowledge, is there such a remarkable transformation of nature as New England in the fall. Reaching a peak in early October, the foliage turns into a veritable riot of color, as the local cliché goes, due to the extraordinary variety of elms, oaks, maples, birch trees, and others that populate the towns and forests. It is a shame that so few Europeans know this America – quiet, gorgeous, civilized, far from the madding crowds of large inner cities. When people ask where I come from, I hesitate (Pittsburgh? Kentucky? Carolina?) and then reply: New England. I often think it should secede from the Union to become an independent state, or else perhaps be annexed by Canada. As Goethe should have said: "New England, Du hast es besser."

It is fitting to confess that I was apprehensive about teaching at a woman's college. But at once I realized that my most urgent concern was simply not to make a fool of myself in the classroom. The students (in the days before Princeton, Yale, Amherst, and other elite schools went co-ed) were extremely bright, and from my first day at Smith to the last I was challenged to meet the standard of excellence they expected of the faculty. This meant working furiously day and often night to keep a step or two ahead of the class by being prepared to the teeth for every session. The fact that the students were all female – except for a few young men who strayed in from other colleges in the Connecticut Valley – proved to be the least of my worries. They were ever attentive, smart, and well read (it seemed they always did their homework), and they were not there to waste time. I look back on my Smith years with great satisfaction and a sense of privilege to have taught such a flock of admirable youngsters. It is a valuable experience to be wished for every fledgling instructor, one that is unfortunately missed by many beginning professors who spend their entire career at a large university.

There is no way adequately to encapsulate ten years of college life, so a single anecdote will have to serve, a story that is true albeit somewhat far-fetched. It was normal at Smith that some of the students were or became celebrities, drawing as the College did from many prominent and wealthy families. In my case that meant standing before famous progenies: everywhere from Molly Ivins to Julie Nixon. Julie was a solid student and a charming girl who twice enrolled in one of my classes. In her senior year, married to David Eisenhower and younger daughter of the President of the United States, she joined a colloquium that concentrated on Karl Marx and Friedrich Nietzsche. During the semester we spent six weeks on the writings of the one and six on the other. At the final session of the class, a group of twelve that met around a large table, I proposed a concluding discussion by asking: now that we have studied the work of the two great dissenters from the great bourgeois consensus of nineteenth-century Europe, which way would you go? Would you be more likely to become a Marxist or a Nietzschean? We went around the table, allowing each student a chance to make a final statement of preference. When Julie's turn came, she chose Marx. Although he was demonstrably wrong on many counts, she explained, at least Marx lived in the Soho section of London and knew the real plight of the poor there, whereas Nietzsche stayed high in the Swiss Alps at Sils Maria and danced abstractly from mountain top to mountain top. It was of course a plausible argument, though probably not the one that might have been expected from an offspring of Richard Nixon. It happened that the President departed only a few weeks later with Henry Kissinger on their famous visit to China, a coincidence that permitted me to proclaim to my skeptical colleagues that he had done so because Julie returned from Smith to the White House and confided to her father: "Professor Mitchell has convinced me that Karl Marx was o.k., so the trip to Peking is a go." Since this last scene is a bridge too far, apologies are due to Julie for inventing it. Yet at least the story does convey something about the intellectual quality of an education shared by students and faculty at a New England institution of higher learning.

The faculty that I found at Smith was simply outstanding, even when one includes several professors whose contribution had more to do with maintaining the gentility there than with scholarly standards. Much of the credit for such excellence is rightly attributed to the former president of the College, William Allan Neilson (as spelling of the middle name indicates, a Scot), after whom the main library is appropriately named. During Neilson's tenure in the 1930s and early 1940s, Smith cleverly attracted a large number of European immigrant scholars and thereby created a notably cosmopolitan teaching corps. It also began to admit Jews to the faculty. In fact, my regular squash partner, Dan Aaron, had been the first Jewish professor at Smith, starting just before the Second World War.

Mention of that name recalls another salient characteristic of life at Smith: its density. Northampton society was composed of a series of tightly woven and intertwining circles. After a couple of years in the Fort Hill apartments, we bought a house at 75 Washington Avenue. The Aarons lived next door until they moved into a dwelling on Paradise Road formerly occupied by the late widow of President Neilson. They were replaced by Peter and Beau Jones, then Bob and Brett Averitt, couples who were often present in our home and always invited to our annual New Year's Eve parties. Right across the street resided the accomplished sculptor Elliot Offner, sweet Rosemary, and their son and daughter. Further down Washington Avenue lived my senior colleague, mentor, and beloved friend Klemens von Klemperer with his wife Betty, a witty and learned professor of English literature. On the next street was the home of Guenter Lewy, whose spouse Ilse was our family pediatrician. Opposite them was the house of the philosopher Murray Kiteley with wife Jean – it was he who kept up my interest in Hume and Hegel. And so on, in a neighborhood where everyone knew everyone through repeatedly encountering others in a variety of settings, both professional and social. This is not even to enter into the thick web of relationships formed by the children of these families, nearly all of whom attended the same public schools of Northampton. So it was, and substantially remains, in small-town America.

The College boasted two extracurricular features of importance to me. One was the faculty club, which offered particularly fine cuisine for lunch and therefore provided a pleasant meeting place with fellow faculty members, including the jovial current President of the College, Thomas E. Mendenhall (alas, a Yalie). One long table was reserved for "singles," affording an opportunity to meet individuals from other departments. If this lacked all the glamour of High Table at Harvard, it created more genuine and lasting friendships. The other feature was the tennis facility, where I soon became part of a regular foursome with Dan Aaron (good forehand), Arthur Mann (adept at the net), and Ramón Ruiz (always aggressive). None of us knew it at the time, but we were all *oiseaux de passage* at Smith: Dan later moved on to Harvard, Arthur to the University of Chicago, Ramón and I to the University of California. But for the time being we participated fully in Northampton's miniature psychodrama of friends and families who kept bumping into one another on the street, at the super market, at school events or public lectures, in the movie theater or the concert hall.

Another significant advantage of the College was ample opportunity to spend more time abroad. Of course there were the summers, which meant that we were regularly freed up by the academic calendar to visit Europe, forays now much facilitated by jet airplane service. In addition, after three years at Smith, I was granted a year's leave in 1964-65 to accept a Rockefeller research grant. We could go anywhere, and we chose Paris.

The reasons were partly personal – my wife favored France, where she had been a student – but also scholarly, since my aspiration to become a Franco-German historian had become clear. After completion of the book on Bavaria (published by Princeton University Press in 1965 and in German translation by Munich's C. H. Beck Verlag in the year following), my attention turned briefly to a survey of French historiography concerning Germany, for which the Bibliothèque Nationale in Paris was perfect. If Freiburg boasts the most stunning cathedral in Christendom, the old BN in the Rue de Richelieu has the most splendid reading room. And also one of the most efficient, where a researcher could plow through one volume after another without pause. Soon, however, my interests drifted back to Bismarck, and I began a study (published in 1971) of the Iron Chancellor's dealings with successive French political regimes from 1848 to 1890, thus spanning Bismarck's entire public career. This little volume, based largely on published French and German diplomatic documents as well as the huge collection of Bismarck's papers known as the *Friedrichsruher Ausgabe*, marked my transition from being a historian of Germany to becoming a card-carrying Franco-German scholar. Unfortunately, there is no identifiable field of Franco-German history in the United States, thus consequently no organization by that name and no journal dedicated to it. In later years, when attending the annual gatherings of French or German specialists in the respective national history of those countries, I always felt like an outsider who was just dropping by for the amusement of those meetings. Paris, however, does have a center of Franco-German studies at the Institut Historique Allemand, formerly located in the ritzy sixteenth arrondissement on the Rue Maspéro and now at a handsome *hôtel particulier* in the Rue du Parc Royal mid-way between the Archives Nationales and the Place des Vosges. There the major journal of comparative Franco-German history is edited, providing an outlet for me to publish dozens of articles and reviews that would have mostly otherwise gone unwritten. For this valuable connection and also the convenience of the IHA's specialized library, I owe a particular debt to the former director Professor Karl-Ferdinand Werner and, more lately, to Dr. Stefan Martens.

During the Smith time I spent three full academic years in Europe: the one mentioned in Paris plus another as director of Smith's Junior Year Abroad Program in Hamburg and a third period of sabbatical leave split among Hamburg, Bonn, and Paris. The Europe that I encountered on those extended trips was undergoing steady and striking change. Not all of it was, in my perspective, for the better. The Vietnam War was heating up, causing a serious deterioration of America's positive image from the immediate postwar years. The Gaullist era was drawing to a close, not before conjuring a pervasive anti-Americanism that made watching the evening television news in Paris a painful exercise. More hesitantly, it seemed, Germany was experiencing something of the same, and I can well recall sitting through emotional student protest meetings at the university in Hamburg when my country was sharply criticized and often vilified. On one occasion I probably contributed in a minor way to this altered mood by delivering a lecture at the nearby Amerikahaus entitled "The Confessions of an American Liberal." My simple argument was that "we" ourselves must bear responsibility for the deepening American military involvement in Vietnam, starting with John Kennedy and Lyndon Johnson, and could not blame it on the conservative Republicans. When I finished, the U.S. consul in Hamburg rose to apologize and to assure that my views were not those of the American government. Yet a substantial number of the audience, including Fritz Fischer, nonetheless came forward to congratulate me. Evidently, my own ambiguity about the war had struck a sympathetic chord. Frequently it was the case, in France as well, that one detected among Europeans far more personal affection and admiration for America than might have been indicated by the current public discourse.

Another evident change in the 1960s was Europe's growing prosperity. In Paris, because the French capital remained largely untouched by the two world wars, that evolution was more difficult to evaluate than in Germany, where inner cities were being refurbished. Hamburg was a champion example of urban renewal. There was no comparison between the devastation I had seen in the mid-1950s and the sparkling facades that were rebuilt a decade later. Indeed, today's tourist passing through the streets of Hamburg or cruising on its waters and canals might scarcely guess that everything there once lay in charred ruins. This one man's judgment is that Hamburg has now become one of the most comfortable and elegant cities in Europe.

Meanwhile, political circumstances were being likewise transformed, although that was not immediately obvious to the outside observer. Most conspicuous was the change of leadership. The reigns of Charles de Gaulle and Konrad Adenauer were finished. During the 1960s in France the presidencies of Georges Pompidou and Valéry Giscard d'Estaing seemed comparatively calm and even-keeled. Much the same may be said of the chancellorships of Ludwig Erhard and Kurt-Georg Kiesinger. In both cases the relative normality of such regimes, including a few scandals, allowed time and space for the growth of European prosperity. A noticeable contrast with Eastern Europe was also emerging. The differences between East and West in terms of political freedom and economic development could not be hidden, and they began to form a large backdrop of discontent behind the Iron Curtain, of which the Prague uprising in 1968 was another telling symptom (after the Budapest insurrection in the previous decade). In the meantime, two names were gaining prominence as potential bearers of a fundamental reorientation. In France it was François Mitterand, who appeared as the Socialist presidential candidate in 1965. Although defeated in that election, he did establish himself as the clear leader of his party, thereby assuring that he would try his luck again against his more conservative opponents. In Germany the person to watch was Willy Brandt – who can forget his *Kniefall* before a Jewish memorial site in Poland? He joined the Kiesinger cabinet as the German foreign minister in 1966. That date marked the early beginning of what was soon known as Brandt's *Ostpolitik*, intended as a more realistic approach to the fact that Germany could now be defined as two states in one nation. This notion, which seemed to confirm the DDR while actually challenging it, was ratified by Brandt's election as Chancellor in 1969. Without question, one can draw a straight line from this time to the destruction of the Berlin Wall two decades later.

Of these lofty considerations I remained fairly well informed through my frequent and long sorties to Europe, during which I did not fail to devour the newspaper press as well as weekly and monthly publications. The minimum was a daily reading of *Le Monde* or the *Frankfurter Allgemeine Zeitung*, the two real postwar papers of record on their respective sides of the Rhine. Much of the information gathered, and therefore one's perception of events, depended of course on location. As already indicated, besides the home base of Northampton, there were three venues of particular importance for me: Hamburg, Bonn, and Paris. In addition, between1961 and 1972, three brief episodes in Europe deserve to be mentioned to round out a picture of the Smith years.

In Hamburg my duties as director of a student exchange program were not unduly taxing. We were comfortably and centrally quartered in the university's guest house on the Rothenbaumchaussee, five minutes from the campus and ten minutes from our daughters' Turmwegschule, which they as fluent German speakers could attend despite some elementary and understandable problems of adaptation. Also, just across the street from our apartment, was a historical research institute, known as the *Forschungsstelle* (directed by the capable and perpetually amiable Dr. Werner Jochmann), where I was awarded an office. It happened that the publication of my first book coincided with the approach of the fiftieth anniversary of Germany's 1918 revolution. As a result, I spent a few sessions with lights and camera being interviewed for a television documentary, and I was invited to teach a colloquium on that topic at the university. These serendipitous circumstances gave the impression, however superficial, of being integrated into the German intellectual community. By the late 1960s, meanwhile, another large research project was taking shape: a three-volume study of the German influence in France after 1870. This undertaking, which was to occupy me for more than a decade, led me to spend weeks at Bismarck's estate in Friedrichsruh, easily accessible from Hamburg, where I labored through manuscripts written in nineteenth-century Gothic script, a torture for any foreign scholar and even for most Germans. At least I received a small reward in the form of a venison lunch (from a hunt on the estate) with the current Fürst von Bismarck (grandson of the Chancellor), a feast impeccably served by a large staff in the dining room of the family residence. It seems altogether unlikely, however, that any of my books were ever shelved in the adjacent library.

The new research project also took me *a fortiori* to Bonn, capital of the Bundesrepublik, where the ministerial archives of the German Foreign Office (*Auswärtiges Amt*) were then located (they are now in Berlin). Again, the Germanic script was a challenge, although his bureaucratic underlings wrote far more legibly than did Bismarck himself, who usually used a large blunt pencil to scratch out an endless succession of memos and marginal comments. It was in Bonn that I learned the true nature of the historian's craft, which is always a battle against infinity. I also came to know and admire a young British scholar, Paul Kennedy, whom I later visited at the University of East Anglia in Norwich before he moved on to a post at Yale. Paul was working on a dissertation concerning German imperialism in the Fiji Islands, a rather provincial topic, I thought, with limited possibilities to expand. How wrong I was. He went on to become one of the most perspicacious historians of his generation, producing a series of large books with vast panoramas of Europe's past and bold predictions about the future decline of America. The point is certainly well taken (as every Brit must know) that all empires must eventually crumble, although it may be a bit premature to pronounce the demise of the USA.

As for Paris, as mentioned, there was the indispensable stop at the Bibliothèque Nationale, not only for the riches and opulence of the main reading room but also to discover the BN's manuscript department. In general, standard French script has remained unchanged across the centuries, and it is quite simple to decipher. The handwriting of Bismarck's counterpart in the 1870s, French President Adolphe Thiers, was unfortunately an exception. Hence the acute difficulties of comprehension presented by his private correspondence easily rivaled those of Bismarck's memos and marginalia. With innate Calvinist persistence, nonetheless, I continued this search of documents at the Bibliothèque Thiers at the Place St. Georges, the President's private residence that was dismantled stone for stone by the Paris Communards in 1871 and then reconstructed under the ensuing Third Republic. Finally, this quest brought me to the entrance (then on the Rue des Francs Bourgeois) and to the interior of the Archives Nationales, France's principal archival repository whose voluminous holdings have nourished much of the rest of my career. Let it be appended that my months in Paris in 1971 also allowed me to renew my acquaintance with Alfred Grosser and to seek out other French specialists in German history such as Georges Castellan, Gilbert Badia, Raymond Poidevin, and Claude Digeon. These names, among others, are proof enough that the French in the postwar era were continuing to keep a close watch on the Rhine, despite the sudden disappearance of the incomparable Marc Bloch, famously executed near the war's end for his part in the French Resistance.

Now to the three brief episodes. The first followed from the chance encounter in the BN, already related, when I bumped into Larry Joseph. He was a frequent resident in Paris, commanding as very few foreigners the language and owning a small apartment at Montmartre in the Rue du Chevalier de la Barre (where I later resided several times during my longer sojourns in Paris). Among his talents, Larry is a champion cyclist, and he proposed that we launch a bike trip to the village where his mother was born in the Hunsrück, a strip of German land nestled between the Moselle and Rhine rivers. Although less gifted, I agreed. With bikes along in the baggage car, we caught a train to Trier and then descended the Moselle Valley before strenuously climbing onto a wooded plateau. There we found the town of Gemünden. We had little information about Larry's ancestors, who – like mine – had emigrated as children to America before the First World War (his father was from Lithuania). We knew only that the family once ran a cattle and horse-trading firm and that now a shoe store with a cobbler's shop stood on the street in front of their small estate. Sure enough, we found the correct storefront and the long abandoned horse stalls behind it. We also met the current residents of the adjoining house, one of whom – a man about our age – recalled standing as a boy at the upper story window on Kristallnacht in 1938 and watching the local synagogue burning. But we soon discovered that the Jews of Gemünden had been well integrated before 1933. In a pub we were introduced to an elderly toothless gentleman who had attended school with Larry's mother. Despite his poor enunciation and strong Rhenish accent, I was able to translate sufficiently as he explained that Jews and Protestants ordinarily received instruction together, whereas Catholic children were often taught separately. Yet the town also had a *Simultankirche*, that is, a church with an altar at one end for Protestants and at the other for Catholics, whereas Jews worshiped separately in that synagogue later ravaged in the Third Reich. These arrangements worked satisfactorily, and Larry's family had departed for the New World not because of anti-Semitism in Gemünden but because the livestock business was declining in an area turning from agriculture to industry and becoming more urban. The most convincing evidence of social integration, however, came from our visit to the still intact Jewish cemetery of the town. It was visibly divided into three sections: early nineteenth century, late nineteenth century, and the period from the First World War to 1933. In the first, all inscriptions were on the eastern side of the headstones and were in Hebrew. In the second, inscriptions were to be seen on both sides, Hebrew on the eastern and German on the western. And in the third, all inscriptions were on the western side in German, bearing names like Johannes, Brigitte, Stefan, and so forth. In short, to judge by this one village, the real story of Jews in the Rhineland was one of steady progressive germanization, not exclusion. So much history in one small place! Thus it is my surmise that before Adolf Hitler became Chancellor, Germany did not so much have a "Jewish question" (*Judenfrage*), as he repeatedly claimed, but definitely it did have a Nazi question.

A second episode worth the mention occurred in 1964 at the annual *Historikertag* in Berlin, a large gathering that is the German equivalent of a convention of the American Historical Association. Through my Smith colleague Klemens von Klemperer I had established contact with the eminent Bonn political scientist Karl-Dietrich Bracher, whose masterful study of *Die Auflösung der Weimarer Republik* had secured his international reputation. My own miniscule claim to fame had to do with the impending publication of my first book on Bavaria, and accordingly I was invited by Professor Bracher to join a panel that he was to chair on the 1918 German revolution. Once on stage, in front of an audience of more than a hundred German historians, I found myself faced with three Young Turks of the profession: Eberhard Kolb, Peter von Oertzen, and Reinhard Rürup. Each was currently advocating a thesis about a potential "third way" that existed in Germany, that is, an attempt to steer a middle path in Germany between the parliamentary system inherited from the Second Reich and the new revolutionary councils (*Räte*) that appeared in 1918 as a middle European response to the Russian soviets. The failure of this effort, in other words, had been a great lost opportunity to advance democracy. My skepticism about that view was expressed in a twenty-minute presentation of the central argument in my book: if any political figure embodied the notion of a third way, it was the Bavarian premier Kurt Eisner, a Jewish Berlin journalist who bizarrely emerged from the revolutionary strudel as the successor to King Ludwig III. It was Eisner who literally proposed a combination of the former Bavarian Landtag and a new Räteparlament. But when it came to a vote in January 1919, Eisner's party of Independent Socialists received only 2.5 percent of the ballots cast. Some way. Not for the first time I was immediately pummeled by my peers, and all I could do was shake my head in disapproval. It was not long before this debate became, as the Germans say, cold coffee, and it is probably accurate to observe that my position eventually prevailed by default after we all moved on to other matters. Only Eberhard Kolb and I were to meet again through our subsequent mutually developed interest in Franco-German relations during and after the war of 1870. In any event, the sensation of the 1964 historical meeting in Berlin was not our panel but the one that featured a clash with daggers drawn between Gerhard Ritter and Fritz Fischer. The latter's extremely harsh rendition of Germany's imperialist ventures before and during the First World War had set the two at odds, and they did not now spare each other's feelings. In essence, Ritter charged that Fischer had slanted the evidence, cherry-picking documents to select only those passages that reflected badly on the Kaiserreich. Fischer maintained that he had merely drawn out the basic truth of the matter by attempting to organize the extensive data, as all historians do, into a coherent and convincing argument. How was one to choose a side? I had come to know and respect both, and certainly each was in his fashion a formidable scholar. Maybe what we needed, in this instance at least, was a third way? Personally my sentiments were rather more closely attached to Fischer, although a residue of ambiguity abides. My student days in Freiburg were not to be forgotten.

Finally, during the later Smith years, I was permitted to make a three-week excursion into the DDR. After passing through a web of border controls in my red VW *Kombiwagen*, I was allowed to choose my itinerary and to circulate freely, provided that I appear each evening at a pre-registered hotel room. My first stop was Dresden (actually my hotel was in nearby Meissen), where I scouted out Saxony's state archives with reference to contacts with Berlin and with Paris in the nineteenth century. This effort did not produce much of note at the time but it did provide the groundwork for my much later investigation of Saxon railways. The most striking individual encountered there was a Herr Schmitt, an archivist with whom I took long strolls from the archive, located on the right bank of the Elbe, across the main bridge to the old town and back. This gave me a chance to observe the incredible destruction left from the war years, including of course the Frauenkirche (now restored), which lay unrecognizable in heaps of rubble. It also allowed Schmitt, without being overheard, to unburden some of his grievances about the prevailing Communist political regime, of which he as a staunch Protestant took a particularly dim view because of the DDR's restrictions on religion. Meanwhile, he loosened up enough to tell me an elaborate anecdote making the rounds in Dresden. It concerned the new East German premier Erich Honecker, who had succeeded Walter Ulbricht in 1971. The details are now half forgotten, but the punch line remains clear. Honecker had inherited a number of serious problems from his predecessor and was setting out to solve them. One was the severe housing shortage in the DDR, for which he had discovered an ideal solution: tear down the Wall. Little did we realize that many years later Ronald Reagan would address those very words to Mikhail Gorbachev.

I moved on to Merseburg, a rather dismal town just west of Leipzig that had the misfortune of being located between the stinking chemical works of Leuna and Buna. I was housed there in the Dessauer Hof, reputed to be one of the very few private hotels in the DDR. From my room I could easily hike up to the castle where an archive had been installed to conserve documents transferred from Berlin during the war. Nearby was the town's only restaurant worthy of the name, where one could order a variety of pork dishes. It was always the same schnitzel: Hawaii-Schnitzel with a slice of canned pineapple on top, Zigeuner-Schnitzel with a roasted red pepper sauce, etc. Decidedly, the DDR was no place for fine cuisine. While working one day in the archives I was handed a note that I was to receive a visitor at the Dessauer Hof that evening. It was a Stasi agent. Since he came with his (silent) wife and consumed a beer during our interview, his appearance did not seem especially threatening. But he was curious about my background and wondered why I spoke fluent German. I thought that I offered him a plausible explanation about my academic training, but apparently that did not suffice to allay his false suspicion that I was also a CIA informer. Weeks later a letter from East Berlin informed me that I was henceforth forbidden to pursue my research in DDR archives, a ban, as it proved, that lasted for the next twenty years. Before leaving Merseburg, along with three other visiting scholars (Swedish, German, and Russian), I drove to Weimar and then over a concrete road – built by slave labor from the concentration camp – to Buchenwald. Little remained of the former killing machine: no more gas chambers or ovens. Instead, a large museum had been erected that was largely dedicated to glorifying the Communist resistance to Nazism (with, for example, a special Ernst Thälmann exhibit). Such a pointed propaganda message was hardly adequate to capture the full reality of the humiliations and exterminations that had taken place in Buchenwald and elsewhere. That larger picture was better brought into focus as we inspected the prison cells and torture rooms of a small bunker near the camp's entrance, a space that had been occupied by the camp's SS guards before 1945. I stood for a while contemplating a long flat table on which inmates were strapped down for beating with a wooden rod.

The last stop on the trip was Potsdam, just outside of Berlin. The town (except for Friedrich II's marvelous castle of Sans Souci) was still quite battered, its streets lined with stumps of buildings and shabby facades. There was a conspicuous presence of armed Russian soldiers who, with automatic weapon in hand, stared twice each day as I nervously passed between my hotel and the local archive. Headquarters of the Russian commandant, as I later learned, were in fact located on the ground floor of the archive building. During my brief visit in Potsdam I made the acquaintance of one of the chief archivists, Dr. Stefan Brather, who cordially (and surprisingly) invited me to dinner at his apartment. There I met his charming wife and their son Sebastian, to whom I presented a small toy truck. Dr. Brather and I sat up late that evening drinking a sour Hungarian white wine, about which he complained at length, yearning as he did for the forbidden vintages of the Rhineland, Italy, and France. After returning to America, I wrote a note to the Brather family thanking them for their hospitality and recalling Sebastian's delight with the truck. It was naïve and foolish of me to do so. Many years later, while working in Berlin's Bundesarchiv (to which the Potsdam documents had been removed in the meanwhile), I was upon request shown my Stasi file, which made reference to my conviviality with Dr. Brather. Obviously my letter had been opened, and he was called to answer for his undue contacts with Western scholars, of which I was only one. In all, five American historians were on the list of those proscribed.

Perhaps these personal recollections will convey some sense of what a divided Europe was like as the Cold War unfolded. Permanent though it seemed, the division was not without its difficulties, tensions, and anomalies. Above all, even the amateur observer could not overlook the discrepancies that were building between East and West. There was always something artificial about the Wall, and I was not alone to conjecture that it would not last forever. Likewise, in the center of Merseburg, stood a colossal statue of Lenin, his hand outstretched into the presumably promising future of the DDR. As the 1970s began, none of us could possibly know that he, too, would soon come tumbling down.

Chapter Five

TRANSITION

It is always delicate to describe the dissolution of a marriage, especially one's own. The story can of course only be told from one point of view, and the dangers inherent in the autobiographical mode are more insidious than ever. The most that can be offered is a personal account that is as straightforward as possible.

Where to begin? Probably best at the time of our first year's leave from Smith College that was spent in Paris in 1964-1965. During that stay my wife became involved with a medical team that was researching the question of "natural childbirth," the so-called Lamaze method. Both of our daughters had been born in that fashion, so Ingrid was already well versed on the subject. Accordingly, she sometimes arose at ungodly hours to attend birth sequences at various Paris hospitals. Once back in Northampton, she began to offer classes in the Lamaze method, so that our dining room was crowded at least one evening a week with expecting couples (the father was required to participate in the proceedings, as had I). In German, she also wrote a book on the topic, *Wir bekommen ein Baby*, which was eventually published by the Rowolt Verlag in Hamburg and was to be found in bookstores throughout Germany. She had discovered a passion. When I then assumed the directorship of Smith's Junior Year Abroad Program in Hamburg in 1968, Ingrid understandably accepted an invitation to join another team at the university hospital, thereby essentially recreating the circumstances of the Paris year. A member of the Hamburg team – we'll call him Frank – was a young medical student with whom she naturally spent considerable time. Simply put, he thereby became a part of her passion.

These seemingly harmless developments were to have consequences unforeseen, at least by me. The fact that handsome Frank was ten years Ingrid's junior raised no red flag for a Smith professor accustomed to dealing on a daily basis with pretty young women students. Just for the record: never during my decade at Smith did I have anything remotely resembling an affair with one of them. This profession of innocence on my part is not necessarily self-flattering, since a reproach that must be made was my lack of sensitivity to the turmoil that was developing in Ingrid's life. Yet no one could have missed her extreme unhappiness upon returning to Northampton, leaving her project behind after the first year in Hamburg. That dissatisfaction was somewhat assuaged by her three-week journey to Germany in the spring of 1970 and by my agreement to spend the ensuing sabbatical year stationed once more at Hamburg University's Gästehaus in the Rothenbaumchaussee. Another less fundamental but doubtless relevant factor was the frequency of my absences for research forays to Bonn and Paris during this second Hamburg year. Meanwhile, Ingrid was again preoccupied with her research team and consequently much involved with Frank. There is no telling how involved at that time. All that is certain was my astonishment when, returning from Paris late in the spring, I found Ingrid packing up her bags – not to return to Northampton, as I assumed, but to store them until the autumn, when she would begin a course of midwifery at the university medical school. I was still absorbing that surprise as we traveled with our two girls to Sweden for a fortnight in mid-summer of 1971, whereupon Catherine, Alex, and I departed from the Stockholm airport after waving goodbye to Ingrid and her sister Gudrun from a porthole window of the plane. The three of us arrived back in America.

The foregoing details should explain as succinctly as possible how it was that I became for the next fifteen months a single parent. The schedule of a college professor is fortunately flexible enough that I could juggle my professional duties and my family chores, a situation with which every single mother or father is perfectly familiar in a nation where nearly half of all marriages end in divorce. That ugly word was not on the agenda, so far as I knew, since we all presumed that Ingrid would return. But when? She did so, as noted, after nearly fifteen months, just before Thanksgiving of 1972. My most striking memory of that moment was her coming into my office in the basement of the Smith College library (recently vacated by Dan Aaron, off to Harvard) and offering to continue the marriage. By that time, however, I had already been interviewed for an academic post in California and my planning no longer included her. I declined. There was one other significant factor, which she did not disclose: Ingrid was three or four months pregnant with Frank's child. I have often shuddered to think of the scenes that would have ensued had I agreed and then learned the whole truth. In that regard, in the interest of full disclosure, let it be added that I had during the past year found a female consort (a graduate student who later married another man and had three children with him), so there could no longer be any justification for me to assume a pose of moral superiority.

In January 1973 I prepared to leave for San Diego, where I had accepted a professorship. On my last evening, the two girls and I watched some old Charlie Chaplin films at the Forbes public library, and then in the snow we walked together for the final time across the Smith campus and said farewell on the corner of Washington Avenue beside our house. As I kissed them goodbye and turned away, it required no refrain of "Danny Boy" to bring the tears. It was the most dreadful instant of my life.

The upshot was a separation that I found hard to bear. In my apartment at La Jolla Shores, just beneath the campus of UCSD where I taught in the daytime, I would lie in the evening for hours staring at the ceiling as if seasick. In the meanwhile, back in Northampton, Ingrid's pregnancy came to term and she delivered a third daughter, Eva. Frank came over from Hamburg for the event and stayed on into the summer. When I returned to Northampton that June, he was living in my house, driving my car, and sleeping with my wife. Divorce arrangements were promptly completed and, as in well over ninety percent of cases in Massachusetts, custody was awarded to the woman. The most that I could obtain was an agreement: Ingrid would be permitted to take the girls to Sweden for a year of schooling there if they could return the following summer and choose whether to continue in Sweden or to remain in America. That was my understanding of the deal as well as the children's, although Ingrid was later to contest it.

In the next academic year, 1973-1974, I resumed my position in La Jolla while Catherine and Alex lived at Lidingö and attended a Swedish school (of which the director was my brother-in-law, Gudrun's husband Arvid Möller, a dear friend of mine). A stroke of luck was determinant. Amherst College, not quite ten miles from Smith, had a faculty opening in European history, and I was invited to spend a year there as visiting professor and possible candidate. UCSD would grant me a leave of absence. Since we still owned the house in Northampton, I consequently had a familiar place to offer my daughters. In the early summer of 1974 they flew from Stockholm to San Diego and, after a brief stay, we drove across the country: Las Vegas (Circus Circus, of course), the Grand Canyon (a painful horseback ride along the rim), Kentucky (Mammoth Cave, Ashland), New England. We were home again, and it would soon be the moment for a decision. Catherine was now fourteen, Alex twelve. Admittedly the situation was ambiguous, since one was of age to choose, the other not yet. In any event, their unmistakable preference was to stay, and that was decisive. To be brief, once they told their mother of the verdict and re-entered Northampton schools in September 1974, she returned and attempted to take them back to Sweden. We went to court again, where my wonderful attorney David Burres had assembled a gaggle of neighbors (Kiteleys, Offners, von Klemperers) who were willing to testify that I was a fit parent. It never came to that. Instead, the judge closed the proceedings shortly after they began by announcing that he would not send the girls back to Sweden in chains. Ingrid and I would have to deal once more. Only this time, de facto, I had been awarded custody. A bargain was struck, including financial arrangements (a time limit on alimony and no more child support, at least for a year), with the proviso that I would send our daughters to Sweden for Christmas and a firm stipulation that they were to be returned to Northampton at the outset of January in time for the resumption of school. Judging from subsequent events, however, it is safe to conclude that Ingrid had no intention of returning them.

Life in Northampton resumed quietly once a settlement had been reached and Ingrid returned to Sweden (where she declined Frank's proposal of marriage and determined to raise her third daughter alone). Catherine and Alex rejoined their old Northampton schoolmates, and I became a regular commuter to the splendid Amherst campus to fulfill my teaching obligations. Again I was a single parent, awkwardly balancing my sometimes competing duties but doing so with relish and relief. For one thing, my girls had become enthusiastic equestrians, so that my chores included ferrying them to and from riding lessons at their Easthampton stables — a task well known to all doting parents. At the same time, as chief cook and bottle-washer, I doubtless left something to be desired: the kids liked to make fun of my hamburger sauce, which they baptized "glop supreme." To compensate for my culinary shortcomings I attempted to mollify them with frequent visits to the take-out counter at Friendly's Ice Cream Parlor.

All of which seemed by now to be quite normal – until December came and I sent the girls, as promised, to Sweden for Christmas. A few days after their departure I received a long-distance phone call. It was Catherine on the line, calling from a girl friend's house to tell me that her mother had confiscated their tickets and passports, informing them that they would have to stay on in Stockholm up to the age of sixteen. What should I do? Please come to fetch us, Catherine replied with Alex at her side.

Therewith began the most chilling James Bond mission of my life. On New Year's Eve Larry Joseph drove me to Logan airport in Boston. There at a bar we sat and contemplated our coming weekend. He was anticipating a visit with a French friend in the suburbs. I was flying to Sweden. On the morning of the first day of 1975 I arrived at the Stockholm airport, took a bus into the city, and caught a taxi to the American Embassy. I had obtained another set of return airline tickets for the girls and had completed the necessary formalities for them to be issued new passports at the Embassy. Meanwhile, after letting their bags out of a window by rope and tramping through the woods of Lidingö, they hailed a taxi and arrived in their little brown fur coats, looking like a pair of downtrodden muskrats. It is, we know, no small matter to leave and in a sense to betray a parent. But they brightened up when their new passports were handed to them, and we sped off in another taxi to the airport. I had considered attempting to leave by ferry to Finland but thought it would prove too slow to allow a safe escape. Time was pressing. I had supposed that our negotiations at the Embassy would take much longer, so our reservations were for an evening flight to London. But when we came to the airline counter, we learned that we might be able to catch an afternoon flight in half an hour. Hurriedly we changed our reservations and checked our bags through to London. Then we hastened up the stairs toward the inspection booths, where all passengers were controlled. Beyond, as we could hear, the engines of our plane were already revving up. The girls entered one booth to the right, I another to the left. It occurred to me that the body search to which I was subjected seemed particularly thorough. It was. As I stepped out into the passenger lounge, I found myself surrounded by five men displaying (but not drawing) pistols. They were not kidding, and I was under arrest.

The girls had been pulled back and escorted to the office of the airport's chief security officer. I was led there to join them.

For the next two hours we were interrogated by the chief, a man whose name I never learned and to whom I shall forever be grateful. He had been tipped off by Ingrid and had several times consulted with her by phone. He was well aware of the seriousness of the situation, which was made plain to me by one of his assistants who displayed a Swedish law book: the minimum sentence for conviction on a charge of kidnapping would be six months in prison. Yet I had two advantages. One was the Northampton court documents, signed by Ingrid and duly notarized, clearly specifying a date certain for the girls' return to America. And, far more important, there was the testimony of the girls themselves, speaking in Swedish to the security chief and making their sentiments known. For his part, he did not feel that he needed to speak to Ingrid again, and fortunately her lawyer was off on a ski vacation in Norway. After what seemed an eternity, he picked up the phone and called the lawyer. Their conversation (which I could intermittently understand) lasted about five minutes, at the end of which he calmly announced: *"Det måste jag gjöra"* (I have to do it). Thereupon he folded up the documents, handed them to me, and simply said: "You are free to go." More tears.

The three of us huddled for a while in an empty waiting room while the security chief arranged to restore our original reservations for the evening flight to London. We arrived there after midnight, stayed at a Heathrow airport hotel, and returned the next day to Boston. His rather more uneventful weekend completed, Larry Joseph picked us up and drove us back to Northampton. There we finished out the academic year without further incident and in the following summer moved together to California. Before leaving I sold the family house on Washington Avenue, and we staged a gigantic yard sale to be rid of untold accumulated junk. Probably I could have remained at Amherst College, but it required no genius to realize that the time had come for a complete change. The transition was accomplished. A new life was about to begin.

All things considered, I am inclined to believe that the outcome was best for everyone concerned. Unquestionably that was true for me. As for the girls, they surely had every right to claim as their own the land and the language in which they were raised. Arguably, even for Ingrid the result was positive. Without having to assuage the disappointment and frustration of two very disgruntled adolescents (with their father in jail?), she moved into an elegant large residence on Lidingö and raised her third daughter, who later presented her with three adorable grandchildren. That said, it was inescapable that someone had to prevail, and in that regard Ingrid was without question the big loser. Her loss can be precisely defined: she was deprived of the privilege, which I enjoyed, of seeing our two daughters growing day by day from cute little girls into beautiful young women.

Freshman at Davidson College

Fulbright student in Germany

New PhD at Harvard University

Director of Smith student exchange in Hamburg

With Herbie in Del Mar, California

Faux Samson in Israel

Slumming in Paris

Catherine and Alexandra

With grandchildren in Colorado

Retired professor, active researcher

Chapter Six

LA JOLLA AND GRENOBLE

Two more different places would be difficult to conceive. One is a swank up-scale California watering hole where ultra-expensive modern dwellings on the hillside above town look out over a flotilla of sail boats and yachts onto the azure blue water of the Pacific Ocean. The other is a rather scruffy architecturally challenged industrial city sunk deep in a river valley ("*dans une cuvette*," as the locals say) surrounded on all sides by steep hills that fold up into the adjacent Vercors, the Chartreuse, and the French Alps. Opposite but not incompatible, these were the locations where I was to spend the next period of my life.

It was the late summer of 1976 when the girls and I reached California. Alex had stayed behind in Northampton to spend a final few weeks with her friends and to care for our cat Kissy, with whom she then flew westward. Meanwhile, Catherine and I drove across the country, she usually at the wheel and thereby putting the thrill back into travel. Along the way we stopped again in Las Vegas at the Hotel Circus Circus, arriving there late in the evening and finding that the only room still available was a bridal suite, decorated garishly in stark red and black. When we went down to dinner about 11 p.m., emerging from our suite, we received a number of dirty looks directed at the old man and his young honey.

Thanks to my ace real estate agent, Peggy Chodorow (wife of my closest colleague at UCSD), I had purchased a small seaside bungalow at 345 Fourteenth Street in Del Mar, the first settlement on the coast north of La Jolla. It was big enough for each of us to have separate quarters,

Allan Mitchell

including Kissy. In addition, we soon acquired a floppy-eared terrier-poodle named Herbie (after Herbert von Bismarck, "the failed son of the Iron Chancellor," as I liked to point out). The girls were immediately put into Torrey Pines High School, located in the interior across Interstate Highway 5, an area at that time largely unsettled (it now has 40,000 residents). Supposedly they were to catch a school bus every morning, but it was not long before I began to hear the vroom-vroom of sports cars owned by local young lotharios who were more than happy to ferry a couple of perky blondes to class. That remark demands a comment. Our appearance in southern California occurred at the height of the "sexual revolution," that is, after introduction of the pill and before the epidemic of AIDS. Careful as I was to supervise my children, curfews and all, there was no rhyme or reason to forbid their dating or overnight parties. We did, however, have strict house rules: no one else stayed over at our place, so there would be no patter of big feet in the mornings. In short, I trusted my daughters, and they earned my trust. As for me, although not to the manner born and ever the Calvinist, I adjusted readily to the prevailing social mores as well but also observed the rules. I took my avocation as a single parent seriously and developed no desire to enter into a second marriage, which never materialized.

Our home in Del Mar was exactly seven miles from the parking lot next to my office building on the UCSD campus in La Jolla. It would ordinarily take about fifteen minutes to drive that distance, depending on the time of day, whereas twenty years later when I left the university it often required forty-five minutes. My regular passenger during that time was Earl Pomeroy, a well published scholar of the American West, whose study of *The Western Slope* remains a classic on the subject. Earl was the departmental chair during the first two years after my return to UCSD. He had been recently widowed, also lived in Del Mar, did not drive, and was therefore always grateful for a lift. He and I often talked shop in my car or at dinner (my reward: he was a great cook), so that I was already thoroughly acquainted with administrative business before my election as his successor in 1978. But I still had much to learn about the nature of bureaucracy. For example, one bothersome aspect of departmental affairs was the chronic disarray of finances, a "leaky pot" as I described it in my inaugural statement as chair to my fellows. Thus, like a good Scot, I set about to tighten the departmental purse strings. By the end of my first year in office I proudly announced to the Vice Chancellor for Academic Affairs, Paul Saltman, that I had succeeded in bringing the situation under

66

control and that the Department of History's annual budget was balanced. "Excellent," he replied, "then you won't need any additional funding for the next year." After that come-uppance I managed to arrange a tidy deficit for the year following.

In other regards, too, I was deficient as an administrator, lacking as I did the necessary skills of diplomacy (possessed in spades by Stanley Chodorow, who became Dean of Arts and Humanities). Two incidents can illustrate the point. On one weekend all the departmental chairs were invited by VC Saltman to an administrative conference held at the fabulous Hotel Del Coronado, famous as the scene of Billy Wilder's clever comedy film *Some Like It Hot.* Imagine, we were walking in the sandy footsteps of Marilyn Monroe! But the whole affair made me a bit uneasy, and I shared with some other chairs my misgivings about our presence in such opulent surroundings at the invitation of the university administration. What was the purpose? Finally, at a plenary session, I blurted out a brief speech to this effect: "We all know there is no such thing as a free lunch. Yet we chairs are rubbing elbows and sharing expensive meals with the top brass of our university bureaucracy. In return they will presumably expect our fidelity. There is every reason for the departmental chairs to cooperate, but there may be times – especially now that a budget crunch in the UC system requires a trimming of faculty and staff – when administrative demands and departmental needs come into conflict. Whenever such is the case, the chairs must side with our colleagues, those who elected us to represent them." Needless to insist, Paul Saltman and others were not pleased with my oration, which they considered to be too frank and unnecessary (as well as ungrateful). Probably they were right.

The other incident arose at a faculty meeting at which the UCSD Chancellor Richard Atkinson (later President of the entire UC system) was attacked by members of the Committee on Academic Personnel for overturning too many of CAP's negative tenure decisions. This prompted another improvisation that went something like this: "I have recently chaired an Ad Hoc Committee of five specialists who met to decide a tenure case. After we all carefully reviewed the file and discussed the matter at length, we voted 4 to 1 in favor of the candidate. As chair of the group, I had the duty of writing a report in which, fairly I thought, I summarized the minority case before explaining the positive verdict. But that decision was then reversed by CAP, which cited my own presentation of the one negative vote, even though it was evident that our Ad Hoc Committee was professionally far more qualified to render a judgment in the case than were members of CAP, who were drawn from a variety of disciplines across the campus. Moreover, in general, statistics showed that CAP had reversed a much higher percentage of Ad Hoc decisions than the Chancellor had nullified CAP decisions. And he had done so almost exclusively in order to secure affirmative action appointments." Again, this statement earned me no kudos from members of CAP or from many other colleagues present. At least Dick Atkinson seemed to appreciate a little support, and he carried on.

Originally I had been brought to UCSD to help build the European wing of the Department. This was the intention of my old tennis partner, Ramón Ruiz, then the chair. We had a solid core: Alden Mosshammer (ancient history), Stanley Chodorow (medieval), David Luft (Austria and intellectual history), and Gabriel Jackson (Spain). Three recruitments in which I had a hand marked an upgrade, especially in the Mediterranean theater. One was John Marino in Renaissance Italy; another was David Ringrose in early modern Spain; and the third was Stuart Hughes. My old mentor was very successful as a fixture at Harvard, but I learned that he was unhappy because his wife Judith had been refused tenure there in French history, despite the publication of her capable monograph, *To the Maginot Line.* With Ramón's blessing, I undertook a trip to Cambridge where I attempted to persuade them that a joint appointment at UCSD was in their future. They agreed. For Stuart it was tit for tat: he had long ago helped me from California to Harvard, and now I was expediting his move from Harvard back to California. The only problem was that CAP, with which I was not on the best of terms, offered to award Judy Hughes a tenure-track position but balked at approving tenure itself. There was only one remedy. I led a delegation of historians to Paul Saltman's office to make clear that UCSD could forget about adding the illustrious Stuart Hughes to the faculty if his spouse did not receive tenure from the outset. Despite any lingering resentment about my unfortunate intervention at the Hotel Del Coronado, that view prevailed and two new appointments were completed. Ah, the joys of university politics.

It would be remiss not to add a footnote. Some months later, still during my chairmanship, another academic tiff occurred over the tenure of my junior colleague and alter ego David Luft, author of a learned intellectual biography of the Austrian novelist Robert Musil. For reasons that escaped me, he was opposed by Hughes and Hughes. With whatever capital that remained, I defended him, as it turned out with success. That outcome produced for me an irreparable strain with Judy Hughes, but not with Stuart. He and I continued our amiable and respectful relationship while he, plagued by a serious heart condition that required two major surgeries, reached the age of eighty. He was still bright and elegant as ever when we lunched at the Faculty Club a day or two after his birthday. But he complained about his growing weakness and died a few months later. My debt to him is obviously considerable, since without his support there would have been in this narrative no Harvard, perhaps no France, and certainly no European section of UCSD's Department of History nearly so superb.

One last note concerning La Jolla involves Herbert Marcuse, at the time also a member of our faculty in the Department of Philosophy. He and Stuart Hughes were good friends, and through that connection I came to know him. Our meetings and discussions were infrequent but sufficient for me to explore the mind of a true Marxist. "True," in his case, meant a Marxism that was drenched with Hegelian thought and that adhered to the orthodox notion that a revolution, which he believed would certainly come, must originate in the industrially most advanced portions of the world. Of these two traits I applauded the first and doubted the second. This mixture of admiration and skepticism went on display one evening when, in the framework of a course I was teaching on modern France, my students and some others gathered to see a documentary film about the insurrectionary events of 1968 in the Latin Quarter of Paris. At the conclusion, after the lights came on, I rose to ask if anyone in the audience happened to be present in France at that time. One hand went up. It was Herbert Marcuse, who had not only been there but who was much involved with Daniel Cohn-Bendit and his band of student rebels. Marcuse held forth for fully half an hour, a spellbinding performance, to everyone's delight. When he finished I could only conclude the proceedings by saying that, while I did not entirely agree with his version that the Paris rioting of 1968 was the harbinger of a coming revolution in Western Europe, I could not possibly top his stirring rendition of it. Enough said.

After two years as the dauphin of UCSD's Department of History and three as its chairman, I was ready for a break. For once, it came as the result of an opportunity long foreseen, carefully planned, and successfully realized. The University of California's Education Abroad Program had a two-year opening in France, an appointment that coincided exactly with the end of my administrative term in La Jolla in 1981. As EAP director in Grenoble, with responsibility for about thirty undergraduates there,

I would also have to supervise programs in Montpellier and Marseille. This suited me in a number of ways. As I was moving on with the third volume of my trilogy about the German influence in France after 1870, the focus of my research had already shifted for a time to Paris. While tending to my duties in Grenoble, therefore, I would be able to travel extensively in southern France and still find the occasion now and then to dip into the Parisian archives. A stroke of fortune was the agreement of EAP headquarters at UC Santa Barbara to purchase a Eurail pass for me, which was the most economical means to acquit my concurrent obligations in Montpellier and Marseille as well as an incomparable convenience for making random side trips. To name just a few of the noteworthy historical sites I visited: Bayeux, Honfleur, Cluny, Beaune, Uriage, Le Creusot, St.-Guilhem-le-Desert, Albi, and (while studying pilgrimages) Paray-le-Monial and Lourdes.

These quick excursions added immensely to my appreciation of France as a land of deep and various historical roots. Heretofore my acquaintance of things French had been confined almost exclusively to Paris. The perception from the provinces is necessarily quite different. Minus the hectic pace of Parisian life, the French seem a much more settled and complacent folk than in the capital. They take time for strolling, shopping (whether in supermarkets, boutiques, or out-of-doors markets), cooking and dining, skiing, swimming, and so forth. These pastimes are often highly ritualized, requiring the observance of habitual patterns, not unlike the French language. In the Midi the ratatouille must be just so and not otherwise, depending on the region. French regionalism is still pronounced, despite the extraordinary degree of centralism exercised by the administration of the national state. The feel of Brittany is quite distinct from that of Normandy, the Rhône (around Lyon) from the neighboring Isère (Grenoble), or the Hérault (Montpellier) from the nearby Bouches du Rhône (Marseille). One has to spend time in those places to pick up their particular rhythm, so unlike the faster beat of Paris, and the EAP directorship gave me the once-in-a-lifetime opportunity to do just that.

My private residence during the two years in France was inherited from my predecessor, whose rather bashed-up car I also took over. The location was in the village of St.-Ismier (pronounced ee-me-ay), about five miles outside of Grenoble. It was a three-bedroom apartment (one used as a study) upstairs with a wrap-around balcony that had a breath-taking view out over the Belledonne, the front range of the French Alps. Downstairs lived my landlady, a Hungarian by birth who was now the widow of her late French husband. Needless to say, we did not speak Hungarian. The village itself was unprepossessing except on Saturday mornings when the local farmers' market appeared with its amazing offering of hand-made wares, including of course all manner of cheese and everything else from olives to sweaters. Even without Freiburg's incomparable cathedral as a centerpiece, the scene was a delight, as were the *saucissons* even though they were maybe not quite in a class with German Bratwurst.

Social life in Grenoble was not conducted, as in Paris, in fancy restaurants, bistrots, nightclubs, or cinema palaces. So where to look? I took a promising initiative by joining a tennis club. There I came to know *la bonne bourgeoisie grenobloise*, which notably included François and Christl Jacquot. He was a native of the region and a physician in Grenoble; she was a Bavarian-born woman from Garmisch, several years his junior, who had come to him for medical treatment and stayed to become his bride. She was the better athlete of the two, and it was more often than not that I rallied tennis balls with her. They lived elegantly in the town of Meylan, between St.-Ismier and Grenoble, also in a house with veranda and majestic view of the Alps. They were, moreover, both excellent skiers and owned a lodge in the resort of Alpe d'Huez, famous for its manicured snowy trails in winter and the fearsome climb by cyclists on one traditional leg of the annual Tour de France in the summer.

A brief comment on each. Alpe d'Huez boasts a large repertoire of ski slopes suitable for beginners and for those, like me, who are experienced but average skiers. Unfortunately, when hosted by the Jacquots, I was expected to tag along with experts. Particularly terrifying was the so-called "tunnel," an abandoned horizontal mine shaft (for what original purpose I never found out) not far from the highest lift station at well over three thousand meters (10,000 feet) of altitude. Departing from the lift, one descended a twisting trail, entered the mine shaft, slithered along while stooping to avoid the low ceiling, and then reached the exit to see … nothing but blue sky. We stood on the edge of a precipice that seemed to drop off at virtually a perpendicular angle. It was possible to inch out a short distance on a ledge to the right, but the moment had to come when there was no alternative to a sharp leftward turn and a plunge down that incredibly menacing slope. For the Jacquots and their ski partners it was all a thrill and great fun. To me it was the closest thing imaginable to suicide. Somehow I managed to survive the ordeal three or four times, so as not to appear cowardly or to disgrace America's fair name, but then – rather like dropping out of a risky police-patrolled parade by the review stand in East Berlin – discretion overcame sinking valor, and I begged off further life-threatening trauma. As for the Tour, we were well placed in the Jacquots' lodge, able to peer from a balcony on the downhill side as the approaching cyclists snaked their way up the steep mountain and then to exit onto the opposite street, just a few yards from the finish line, to watch them bobbing and weaving toward the climax. This was definitely more my kind of thrill, safely observing the proceedings from the sideline with the accustomed passive posture of a professional historian, calm and objective. What interested me actually were not so much the half dozen top finishers who breezed by effortlessly, it seemed, without much visible strain. Rather, the true spectacle was the awful procession of stragglers who were laboring mightily through the punishing final meters, their eyes bulging, their faces marked by acute pain, and presumably their legs cramping from exertion. Decidedly, as my mother would have said, Alpe d'Huez was no place for the fainthearted.

The University of Grenoble is probably one of the better educational institutions of provincial France, especially reputed for its science faculty (with which special ski and tennis institutes are affiliated). But the humanities, where most of our California students were enrolled, were perhaps less distinguished, and certainly there was nothing there to match the towering prestige of the scholars by whom I had been taught at Sciences Po in Paris. Most of what I know about regular campus life came from my conversations with our exchange group. Our students were struck by the lack of any real connection with their professors in the classroom or elsewhere. The French faculty members would come to the lecture hall for a formal fifty-minute presentation of a highly structured subject. Their French students arrived with a fist of colored pencils, which they would deploy alternatively to create an outline of the lecture, with major headings in one color, subheadings in another, and additional comments in a third. There was rarely a question from the class or any discussion of concepts advanced from the lectern. I have no way of judging how typical this impression was, or how close to reality, but that was the majority view. Consequently, the UC program organized small tutorials for our EAP students and thereby, in effect, engaged a supplementary junior faculty who provided the prompting and coaching absent in the classroom. As director I was of course nominally in charge of this operation, but most of the credit was due to my French administrative assistant (who also handled some correspondence and kept the books). For Marie-Hélène Sénéchal, "lovely" is just the right word, not to mention her intelligence and street smarts. As an added bonus, her husband Jean was a physician to whom our students could turn at any time with their medical problems. Together, we ran a tight ship.

In sum, the EAP program in Grenoble proved to be both satisfying and successful. The same could not be altogether claimed for the annex program in Montpellier. There were two basic problems. One was propinquity. Although I loved the charming town of Montpellier, I only managed to appear there every other week and could not sustain the same contact as in Grenoble. Furthermore, whereas the Grenoble office was located right at the center of the campus, in Montpellier it was eccentric (near a Roman aqueduct), forcing the students to make a cross-town trip to reach it. As a result, they came by irregularly, if at all, and were too frequently left to their own devices. Some thrived well enough on such a regime, others not. It was surely evident that the thirty-some students in Montpellier deserved to have their own director as well as a bureau nearer to campus. Yet my complaints to the Santa Barbara headquarters went unheeded. The other problem was personal. My administrative assistant in Montpellier was a much less gifted person than Madame Sénéchal and could not be counted on for much initiative or regularity in caring for our charges there. Far worse still, near the outset of my second year on the job, she and her husband were killed in an automobile accident. To say the least, this horror created a disruption not easily overcome. Our program in Montpellier consequently limped to the finish line, rather like one of those straggling cyclists on the Tour de France. As for the third contingent of our program in Marseille, to which only five or six students were attached, that went swimmingly within the tight boundaries of a well organized curriculum of marine biology. My occasional visits there were sufficient to keep the independent-minded Marseille group on even keel.

One other activity during these two years merits a special mention. During the preceding stretch while I was chairing the Department of History at UCSD, a visiting professor was temporarily brought in to join our program in Judaic Studies. Yigal Shiloh was a world-famous archeologist in charge of a major dig in the most ancient settlement of Jerusalem, outside the walls of the old town, known as the City of David. I came to know him and his dynamic wife Tamara quite well, and they invited me to visit them in Israel. As it turned out, this was the first of four trips there in the late 1980s. Except for the last of these, when I stayed for the most part at a Club Med on the Red Sea at Elath, I ordinarily lived in the Shilohs' basement, worked along with a batch of other amateurs

– mostly American college kids – at the dig, and accompanied Yigal to various other archeological sites throughout Israel. It was an education. As I wrote in dedicating one of my books to him, Yigal Shiloh was the one who taught me the difference between the nineteenth century B.C. and A.D. Meanwhile I became closely acquainted with Tami's mother Liselotte, always called Lilo, whose family had wisely left Cologne already in 1933 to take refuge in Palestine. She showed me around the port cities of Akko and Haifa, where she lived, and she visited me in Grenoble, where she was especially delighted by an excursion to Annecy. Like her son-in-law, she taught me much about the history and the current reality of a part of the world that I had previously known only from a Bible class. Both of these remarkable individuals tragically disappeared at the end of the decade: Yigal, prematurely, the victim of a cancer; and Lilo, at about the same age as my mother in her mid-nineties, from an age-related malady. They remain sharply etched in memory.

Most of the foregoing was focused on France. This concentration was appropriate at a time when I was entering the final stages of my trilogy on the German influence in France after 1870. The second volume, published in 1984, concerned reform of the French army and of public education, both adapted, albeit differently, from German models. That research had taken me as far afield as the Vatican archives and, as mentioned, a pilgrimage to Lourdes. The third volume, centered on social reform, would also require extensive investigation in France, but I saw a need to return to Germany in order to gain a firmer understanding of the Bismarckian social welfare system. That effort would determine my next steps.

Before turning back to Germany and the tumultuous changes that were soon to occur there, let it be recalled that France was also undergoing an exciting evolution because of the new Socialist regime inaugurated by François Mitterand in 1981. After the initial defeat of his presidential candidacy in 1965, he made a second attempt in 1974, only to be narrowly defeated by Giscard d'Estaing. Not long thereafter, to insert a brief flashback here, I was a visiting member of the faculty at Amherst College. Through a professor in Amherst's Department of Political Science with whom he had personal connections, Mitterand received an offer to appear at the College, which he accepted. Defeated, he was still unemployed. Naturally, I was eager to hear him in person and asked Larry Joseph to join me. We sat only a few rows back in the college chapel as Mitterand delivered a rather flat oration in French about the possible future of a united Europe. After the polite applause had died, we trundled across the campus to the residence of the college president, who was staging a reception for Mitterand. As a visiting faculty member (who was teaching French history), I was invited. We entered the large central salon to find Mitterand seated in a large Windsor chair while several students and young professors crowded around to pose questions as if they were a press corps. When it came my turn, I asked in a brisk tone: *"Maintenant que votre carrière politique touche à sa fin, qu'est-ce que vous pensez faire dans l'avenir?"* (Now that your political career is approaching its end, what do you plan to do in the future?). Mitterand fixed me with a stare – an expression I later observed more than once at his televised press conferences when some reporter asked him a particularly stupid or impertinent question – and fluttered his long dark eye lashes, as he was wont to do before giving a properly dismissive response: he would certainly find some way to serve his country.

When François Mitterand was finally elected to the French presidency in 1981, he proved yet again that I had better stick to history and not prophecy. The jubilation and wild ovation of the huge crowds in France was much like those in America years later that celebrated the victory of Barack Obama. In both cases, many people expressed their unrestrained enthusiasm at turning out a more conservative regime and embracing the promise of change. His previous setbacks not withstanding, Mitterand proved to be a strong and willful president for more than a decade before his death. Paradoxically, in some ways he was the most de Gaulle-like of those to hold that office after the General himself, specifically including his major construction projects in Paris such as the bunker-like building of the new hyper-modern Bibliothèque Nationale de France at Bercy and the monstrous Grande Arche that straddles the plaza of la Défense at the Porte Maillot. Arguably his most important test, however, concerned the further development of the European Union. As always, at least since 1870, France had to face the German question.

Chapter Seven

BIELEFELD AND BERLIN

Initially, after my return from France to the United States in the early autumn of 1983, my focus remained fixed on the French side of several new problems arising from the third volume of my trilogy, the one that was to treat nineteenth-century social reform. After serving (including my EAP tour of duty in Grenoble) at the University of California for seven consecutive years, I was in the enviable position of possessing a large quantity of sabbatical credits, which enabled me henceforth to spend half of my time in Europe. Personal circumstances were also propitious, since my daughters had finished high school in Del Mar and were safely parked elsewhere for their future education: Catherine at Mills College in Oakland CA and Alex at the University of Colorado in Boulder. In Paris I was able to occupy Larry Joseph's neat apartment on the slopes of Montmartre during the academic year when he was teaching at Smith. In addition, through him, I met a remarkable woman who made me an offer I could not refuse. Chantal Bamberger was a radiologist at the prestigious Hôpital Foch on the edge of the Bois de Boulogne. A person of many interests and talents, among them the piano, she was an avid patron of the arts and above all the opera. Her husband, Dominique Bozo, had meanwhile established himself as a maven in the Paris art world, becoming director of the Pompidou Center (France's most visited tourist attraction) and administrator of the new Picasso museum. Dominique's premature death from cancer left Chantal to preside over a spacious apartment on the Rue du Vieux Colombier, hard by the Place St.-Sulpice, as well as a rambling country estate in Normandy. With her three grandchildren and three rowdy dogs, she retreated as often as possible from apartment to estate in the summers and during Easter vacations. Since she had collected museum-quality paintings in her Paris flat, however, she was uneasy about leaving the place unoccupied during her absences, and accordingly she wondered if I could help her out by living in the apartment when she was in Normandy. *Quel sacrifice de ma part!* This arrangement was to last through many years, and it is certain that without it I could not possibly have sustained the pace of my research, for which my gratitude is beyond any bounds. It remains a personal debt that can never be repaid.

It may be of interest to list briefly some of the places a scholar must seek out in Paris in order to investigate social history. Indispensable, of course, are the usual *bonnes adresses* of the Archives Nationales and the Bibliothèque Nationale. In addition, one needs to scout out the archives of the French Academy of Medicine in the Rue des Saints-Pères near St.-Germain des Prés, the Archives de Paris at the Porte des Lilas, the Archives de la Préfecture de Police (formerly on the Quai des Orfevres where Georges Simenon's Inspector Maigret had his office), and the Foreign Office archives at the Quai d'Orsay. Less obvious but equally important are two other repositories: the Musée Social, on the Left Bank just off the Boulevard St.-Germain, and the Service de la Documentation et des Archives de l'Assistance Publique de Paris, situated in the Rue des Minimes only a block from the spectacular Place des Vosges. Of necessity, driven to piece together the complexities presented by the scraps of paper I found in these various locales, I spent many hours in each of them. If I may quote from the preface of my resulting study – after a reference to my family background of Scottish immigrants – I wrote: "These circumstances help to explain a certain passion that I have brought to my research and writing. Not only do I hold that a society is obligated to offer equality of opportunity to citizens of every origin, I am also persuaded that politics should serve to promote that ideal, however unattainable it may be in practice. I therefore believe in the necessity of state intervention to deal with social problems. It is this premise, and not a preference for Germany over France, that has colored my judgment about events in Europe. Surely no American in my lifetime has any reason to observe with smugness the difficulties of late nineteenth-century France. Insofar as social policy is concerned, the parallels between the French republic then and the American republic now are impossible to ignore. It affords little comfort to conclude that, a full century later, the United States has barely attained the level of the early Third Republic in crucial matters of public health and welfare." Disgracefully, those words were no less valid after another twenty years as the government of Barack Obama struggled to pass meaningful social reform to bring health insurance to all American citizens.

In the quest for a history of social legislation there were two symptomatic topics that particularly drew my attention. One of them was alcoholism. As in most European countries, this scourge became much more prominent in France during the late nineteenth century, spurred as it was by improved railway transportation that permitted increasing quantities of cheap wine and hard liquor (such as lethal calvados) to be distributed nation-wide. By the turn of the twentieth century France alone had over 30,000 wholesale distributors of alcoholic beverages and thereby provided a bar for every eighty-five inhabitants or, more tellingly, one drinking locale per thirty adult males. The implications were obviously enormous for French taxation policy and for the growth of political lobbies opposing state regulation or financial reform. But most urgently of all it was a health issue. To deliver a paper on that topic, I was invited to a conference in Rome. One of the organizers of it was my former undergraduate student at Smith, Susanna Barrows, whom I had come to know closely during my year at Amherst while she, after receiving her Ph.D. at Yale with Peter Gay, was a professor at Mt. Holyoke College. She was one of the most delightful human beings I ever met. Already author of a fine study of theories about crowd behavior in France after the Paris Commune of 1871, called *Distorting Mirrors*, Susanna (who soon moved on to UC Berkeley) had also become an expert in the history of French cafés. Unsurprisingly, like most participants at the conference, she had a highly developed palate for good wine and excellent cuisine, so that our week in Rome was hardly wasted in that respect. Easily the highpoint, however, was an hour-long audience with Pope John Paul II at the Vatican. The conference group of about fifty scholars was ushered into a small auditorium with a podium at one end. A member of the pontiff's staff placed a manuscript on the lectern and then stepped aside as the Pope in his robes entered and began to read from it. Delivered in a soft monotone English, the text was scarcely comprehensible (reminding me of Gerhard Ritter's lectures in Freiburg), but the message was clear and just what the conference members wanted to hear: alcohol should be consumed only in moderation. After all, it would have been unseemly for a Polish pontiff to preach total abstinence amid the vineyards of Italy. At the conclusion John Paul lifted his right hand with three fingers extended and made the sign of the cross. It was the second and doubtless final papal blessing of my life.

The other major topic was tuberculosis. Like alcoholism, TB reached epidemic proportions in late nineteenth-century Europe. But then, after the First World War, it began to abate. Why was that so? This question was the focus of another academic conference I attended in Kassel at the invitation of Christoph Sachsse and Florian Tennstedt, two of Germany's leading experts on the subject of social reform. The debate raged around the so-called McKeown thesis, according to which in effect an "invisible hand" passed over Europe that instigated a decline of the epidemic as if by natural causes – aided to be sure by antibiotics, improved nutrition, and better public housing. Most of the participants supported this view and hence vociferously opposed the notion that state-sponsored public health measures had much to do with the improvement. I was in the minority, since my paper claimed to uncover a fatal flaw in the argument advanced by McKeown. He, like nearly all those attending the conference, had failed to study or take seriously the case of France. The fact was that the French were afflicted, both before and after 1918, by a TB mortality rate nearly twice that of Germany. Why, then, did the invisible hand neglect to pass over France? My proposition was that state intervention made the difference, in Britain ordinarily at the municipal level, in Germany more often organized nationally. Before 1945 France had no national health care system of the sort adopted by Germany under Bismarck. The only health insurance program offered to the French population was through mutual aid societies (called friendly societies in Britain), which were privately operated, generally small in membership, and too expensive for most persons to afford. Moreover, they usually did not admit subscribers who had a pre-existing condition such as tuberculosis, lest they break the bank. At the same time, Germany had a public system of health insurance that directly or indirectly covered over half of the population. This had encouraged the expansion of medical schools (admired and often attended by Americans), greater specialization of the medical profession, and in particular the growth of a sanatorium movement virtually unknown in France. In German hospitals TB patients were normally isolated or at least separated into special wards; in France, all too frequently not. For these reasons, among others, the title of the third volume of my trilogy was *The Divided Path*.

Admittedly, after completion of my research in France, it was clear that I needed to investigate more thoroughly the social legislation of Bismarckian Germany. The opportunity to do so came unexpectedly in the spring of 1986 when, in California, I received the visit of Jürgen Kocka. A few years younger than I, Kocka was already an established figure in the "Bielefeld school" of scholars, a small group that had coalesced around Kocka and Hans-Ulrich Wehler and that was considered the cutting edge of social history in Germany. Kocka was in the midst of organizing a gigantic year-long research project at the Zentrum für Interdisziplinäre Forschung (ZIF) in Bielefeld, which would be devoted to a comparative international study of the European bourgeoisie (*Bürgertum*) in the nineteenth century. He invited me to join this team of scholars, and without any hesitation I accepted. My university granted me three quarters of leave, and I was off to the ZIF.

Bielefeld does not rank as one of Germany's premier beauty spots. The town is quite plain and humdrum, sitting between Münster and Hanover in a drab northern landscape that lacks any vistas of lakes or mountains. Nearby, at least, is the Teutoburger Wald, not inconsiderable but less impressive by far than the Black Forest and without the latter's sprinkling of charming villages. The University of Bielefeld is of relatively recent vintage, post-Second World War, and is architecturally notable for being housed in a single huge edifice that resembles an outsized airplane hangar. Close by is the ZIF, a separate village of its own consisting of small concrete bunkers that serve as housing for visiting fellows and a large central meeting hall for seminars and lectures. The ensemble is completed by a dining hall and quarters for the administration. If this sight is less than thrilling, the assembly of research scholars gathered by Kocka from all corners of Europe was about as impressive as one could conceive. After the conclusion of that academic year, 1986-1987, three volumes of essays were published by an all-star cast that included, for example, Eric Hobsbawm from Britain, Marco Meriggi from Italy, Bo Stråth from Sweden, Györgi Ránki from Hungary, Patrick Fridenson from France, Henk van Dijk from the Netherlands, Waclaw Dlugoborski from Poland, Hannes Siegrist from Switzerland, and Hartmut Zwahr from the DDR. This incomplete listing suggests the variety of scholars in attendance for shorter or longer periods, although it omits numerous distinguished names from Israël, the United States, and especially West Germany (starting with Hartmut Kaelble, Dieter Grimm, Ute Gerhard, Heinz-Gerhard Haupt, Dieter Langewiesche, and Ute Frevert). My apologies are due to the others whose written contributions are to be found in that three-volume edition of essays issued by the Deutscher Taschenbuch Verlag in 1988.

Although Hans-Ulrich ("Uli") Wehler was not formally enrolled in the ZIF project, his presence was significant for everyone concerned. I had first met him and his wife Renate years before while he was still an assistant of Theodor Schieder at the University of Cologne. Since then he had published several controversial books that established him as an international star, and he was launching his massive five-volume study entitled *Deutsche Gesellschaftsgeschichte*, which was to track the development of German society from 1700 to the present. His work, which went through a succession of theoretical incarnations, was of particular interest to me because at one point he had formulated a thesis about Bismarck's Bonapartism to which I was forced to take exception. To simplify, in a first phase Wehler chose a British model for his *Das deutsche Kaiserreich 1871-1918*, published in 1973. The story was that imperial Germany, unlike Great Britain, had not undergone a fundamental social transformation, with the result that German democracy, saddled with an essentially feudal ruling system that remained unmoved, was unable to produce a viable modern society. This thesis received severe criticism from a pair of young English historians (both of whom emigrated to professorships in the United States), Geoff Eley and David Blackbourn. When Blackbourn appeared very briefly in Bielefeld, he and Wehler stood on the platform together and tried to outdo each other in attempts to reach common ground. Wehler had already abandoned the British model and moved on to a second phase of construing French Bonapartism during the Second Empire (1851-1870) as the inspiration for a Bismarckian "plebiscitary democracy." Although I was a Wehler fan, this notion did not slide easily down the gullet. To start with, Bismarck's position as chancellor was rather more like a figure such as François Guizot before 1848, that is, the dominating first minister of a figurehead on the throne. Beyond that, the last thing Bismarck would actually have attempted, as did Napoleon III, was a plebiscite. How would he have fared in Bavaria, the Rhineland, and heavily Catholic pockets of Silesia during the Kulturkampf in the 1870s? Or in Berlin, the Ruhr, and any other industrial area in Germany during his unsuccessful anti-Socialist campaign in the 1880s? Wehler's thesis could not fly, and he abandoned it as well. It is pleasant to report that, in the third volume of his encyclopedic social history and also in a more recent biography of Adolf Hitler, he has returned home to embrace Max Weber as the proper model-giver for German history.

Joined at the hip with Wehler as a proponent of the Bielefeld school, Jürgen Kocka was in fact a quite different animal. Or, to mix metaphors, he came across more like rich red wine to Wehler's sparkling champagne. Kocka is a born manager: even-tempered, warm-hearted, affable, widely read, conciliatory, commanding but not bullying, a good listener and a fluent speaker. Like Wehler (who studied at Ohio University), Kocka's first main international connection was to the United States, where he was once a student at the University of North Carolina in Chapel Hill. Intellectually, apart from the inevitable Max Weber, his lodestar has been American sociology of the sort professed in the mid-twentieth century by scholars like Talcott Parsons. His career – continued after Bielefeld at the Free University in Berlin – was propelled by his extensive research on the German industrial giant Siemens-Halske. This study provided bedrock and many of the structural elements for later synthetic works, for instance, his influential volume on German functionaries, *Die Angestellten in der deutschen Geschichte 1850-1980*. His conspicuous talents as a synthesizer have gone hand in hand with his many activities as an academic manager, all of which were put to good use in Bielefeld's ZIF project and later in a series of administrative positions in Berlin. For someone like me, who enjoys and/or suffers from the reputation of being an archive rat, there is only one bone to pick: Kocka's given orientation and his multifarious public duties have largely precluded the kind of research into primary sources that are so essential for an archival scholar. When asked, Kocka has offered that such labor is best left to graduate students who are guided by their older and more experienced senior professors and who then reciprocate by making the result of their findings available to them. Such teamwork is of course common on both sides of the Atlantic, especially in the hard sciences, but it is bound to be different from the kind of Lone Ranger research to which I had become accustomed. In any event, the Bielefeld year was a godsend, enabling me to become personally acquainted with many of Europe's leading authorities in social history and to round out research for the third volume of my trilogy, at last published in 1991.

The attention to Germany, as is evident from all of the above, was primarily academic rather than political. Yet political stirrings in Europe, though only dimly perceived by most of us, were becoming evident. There were some hints of this activity from our Eastern European colleagues in the Bielefeld group, and in one crucial regard a limitation was thereby imposed on our proceedings. As the ZIF year wore on, a few others and I became disturbed by the lack of direct reference in our discussions to Marxism, surely the most important theoretical appraisal of the European bourgeoisie in the nineteenth century. Naturally, because he was sensitive enough to avoid any embarrassment to the East European fellows he had invited to join the Bielefeld project, Jürgen Kocka was steering away from that topic. But at one session the Leipzig historian Hartmut Zwahr delivered a paper on the relationship between the bourgeoisie and the working class. If ever there was a moment to compare approaches of the Bielefeld group to the Marxist interpretation, this was it. Accordingly, I asked Zwahr to comment on that problem. Visibly discomforted, he attempted only a brief statement in reply before Kocka smoothly and diplomatically changed the subject. As it turned out, Hartmut Zwahr was shortly to become a leader and a hero of the popular unrest that erupted in East Germany, of which the epicenter was Leipzig. No wonder he was reluctant to express his views openly and prematurely in answer to my question. That said, it seems only fair to concede that a weakness of the Bielefeld survey was a failure adequately to grapple with orthodox Marxist theory. In at least two regards our deliberations importantly diverged from it. First, the prodigious collective learning of our participants far better illustrated the nuances of national differences among the European middle classes than did the writings of Karl Marx. And second, the Bielefeld analyses more lucidly revealed the various layers of bourgeois status groups. Whereas Marx tended to caricature the bourgeoisie as bankers and businessmen who ruthlessly exploited the working poor for their own profit, the Bielefeld image was more variegated, examining social elements from wealthy entrepreneurs to modest shopkeepers and also not ignoring the significant presence of a *Bildungsbürgertum*, meaning all manner of artists, intellectuals, lawyers, university professors, and so forth. This is not to mention bourgeois women, about whom Marx had virtually nothing to say. A few years later I met with Jürgen Kocka in New York, where he asked me to assist him in editing an abridged English anthology of the Bielefeld essays and to write an introduction for it. I did so, but my opening paragraphs included an expression of my disappointment that a comparison with Marxist theory was nowhere fully treated. Jürgen Kocka requested that those remarks be deleted, and they were.

For reasons both professional and personal, Berlin was meanwhile becoming a center of my operations. That began as usual with the archival resources located there, notably the vast holdings of the Bundesarchiv, housed in a former army base near the Free University, and the Prussian state archives in the suburb of Dahlem, also nearby. Besides Jürgen and Urte Kocka, my main contact in Berlin was the Swiss couple of Hannes Siegrist and Lilli Sprecher, who had been my regular sauna partners at the ZIF in Bielefeld and who generously took me in from time to time at their apartment in the Blissestrasse. Hannes was completing a whopping

600-page study comparing members of the legal profession in Germany, France, Italy, and Switzerland. Lilli had a mother living in the Engadine valley south of St.-Moritz, to which I was also invited. There her family home was situated in the village of Vicosoprano, as the name indicates, only a few kilometers from the Italian border. Besides that delight, I was led to a neighboring village where the house stands that was the scene for Johanna Spyri's famous children's novel *Heidi*, which I had unknowingly read at the age of twelve in my old Kentucky home, far, far away. The Bielefeld connection also contributed another useful contact in Berlin at the Historische Kommission (called HIKO), a housing and office complex with a library on the Nicholassee in the extreme West End of Berlin, not far from Potsdam (still off limits to me). With the assistance of the historian Stefi Jersch-Wenzel, who had roomed in the same building as I at the ZIF, and the award of a Fritz-Thyssen fellowship, I was able to put up there on three different occasions in the late 1980s.

Berlin had one further attraction, about which I must be discreet. A few years earlier, when I returned one Christmas from Europe, I encountered a new friend who could aptly be described as a Berlin beauty (an appropriate expression at a time when the American press was discovering the German *Frauenwunder*). Her husband was a visiting professor at UCSD, and she had found there a temporary post as instructor in the Department of History. Her academic credentials were solid: she had published a perceptive monograph on French feminist literature in the late eighteenth and early nineteenth centuries, later to be expanded into a definitive full-length study of that topic in French, published in Paris at the Institut Historique Allemand in 2001. We thus became acquainted as professional colleagues in California, but when I returned to Paris in the following autumn, the relationship became closer. She visited there and traveled with me to several other sites in France, among them Reims, Chartres, and the magical castle of Chenonceaux in the Loire Valley. Thereafter I saw her frequently in Berlin while staying in the Blissestrasse, the HIKO, or the Schlosshotel Gehrhus near the Roseneck. I know of nothing further to say other than that I was in love, as she also seemed to be. For her, however, our relationship had limits. When I proposed that she join me in California, she declined. Instead, almost miraculously at age forty-two, she bore a son, the love of her life, and she remained in Berlin to raise him. Nearly two decades later she and the boy, by then a strapping university student, visited me in Colorado. For a week we caught a glimpse of what might have been but never was. I treasure a photograph of her sitting before a crackling open fire in my study.

Although I was prevented from entering any DDR archives, when in Berlin I was allowed to cross over at the Friedrichstrasse underground station into East Berlin. Out of curiosity, I did so often despite the tiresome formalities and the extracted fees for a visa. No one who compared the two sides of the city could have overlooked the disparities that continued to develop between East and West. Yet I can claim no more than very faint intimations of the DDR's fragility and mortality. It must be sobering in retrospect that all of us in the West, even specialists in European affairs, were largely ignorant of the potential for roiling agitation that was soon to occur in Poland, Czechoslovakia, and East German cities like Leipzig. But that slow fermentation was already spreading, a silent but powerful process that was eroding the base of the Berlin Wall and that would, in November 1989, bring it down.

Chapter Eight

REVOLUTION AND RAILWAYS

An argument can be made that 1989 was a more important year than 1789. Thousands of historians have made a living from interpreting the causes, course, and consequences of the French Revolution. But what did it actually accomplish? In posing that question one must by all means avoid what the British philosopher (who taught at Harvard) Alfred North Whitehead once called "the fallacy of misplaced concreteness," that is, ascribing an active historical role to an abstract concept – as if, for instance, we were to say that the Enlightenment produced Voltaire, Montesquieu, and Rousseau. The French Revolution, we know, did not actually *do* anything. It just was. But what was it? Not, to follow the lead of eminent historians like Alfred Cobban and François Furet, the overthrow of feudalism by a united and insurgent entrepreneurial capitalist bourgeoisie. Their convincing suggestion is that no fundamental reordering of European society occurred in the wake of the Revolution – to accomplish that would require the long and repeatedly upsetting turmoil of the entire nineteenth century. Instead, what the decade after 1789 represented was a challenge to Absolutism, which assumed the rather obvious form of beheading Louis XVI. If so, Napoleon Bonaparte can be seen as the last hurrah of a claim to dynastic rule, and the century thereafter may be portrayed as a period of political strife, a perpetual struggle between divine right and parliamentary democracy.

If this compressed and thus simplistic scenario is anywhere near the truth, then it stands in contrast to the events of 1989, which abruptly and (so far as we can tell) decisively altered the topography of Europe. The seemingly immutable division of the Continent into eastern and western spheres was suddenly terminated, to be replaced by an imperfect but vital European union, a comity of nations in which many old borders and even older prejudices were displaced, and in which armed conflict (the Balkans, as usual, were at least temporarily exceptional) among states has become virtually inconceivable. Since 1989 there has never been a better time to be a European. The avowed twin goals of every statesman, peace and prosperity, have been realized as never before in what can only be described as a European Revolution.

For such dramatic change the stars were most propitiously aligned. First, after the heroic but abortive uprisings of East Berlin (1953), Budapest (1956), and Prague (1968), another wave of popular agitation was in progress — notably at the shipyards of Gdansk, whence the prototypical Polish worker Lech Walesa emerged. Second, crucially, Germany had just the right set of lead actors: an aging and ill party boss, Erich Honecker, in the DDR; and the stolid and steady if unspectacular Helmut Kohl as Chancellor of the West German Federal Republic. Then there was the pair of chief representatives from the two Cold War superpowers, each also perfectly cast for his role: in the Soviet Union the reform-minded Mikhail Gorbachev, resembling no one so much as the Dutch boy trying to stop a spillage by putting his finger into a dike; and the somewhat bumbling but eminently sensible American President George H. W. Bush. If there was a bit player who appeared slightly out of step, it was François Mitterand, who (like many other Europeans) was well enough pleased with a divided Germany and who was counting on the USSR to keep matters under control; he was at most a belated convert to German reunification. True, none of these individuals was free of ambiguity about the circumstances that unfolded. Yet they responded as one to the operative factor: a signal from Moscow that this time there would be no Russian military intervention to quell the rising tide of dissatisfaction in Central Europe. Hence there would be no Tiananmen Square in Leipzig. Once that became clear, the rest inexorably followed.

According to one of my small pocket calendars (always carried on travels for the past forty years) for 1989, I had already visited Berlin three times that year before November, albeit for reasons professional and personal rather than political. Living and researching in Paris that autumn, I was already planning a fourth trip in mid-November when breaking news on television began to present images of excited public demonstrations and serious disorder in the East. Then came the incredible pictures of November 9, now so familiar, as German students danced and screamed for freedom atop the Berlin Wall. Two days later I left for Germany, stopping briefly to visit friends in Bremen and arriving in Berlin on November 13, four days after the *Mauerfall*.

Along the way, from the train window passengers could see the extraordinarily animated railway terminals where refugees stood with suitcases and bags stuffed with whatever belongings they could manage to carry. First stop was the Bahnhof Zoo, then West Berlin's central station, a block from the Kurfürstendamm. There, spilling out onto the streets, flocks of people were milling about, many of them East Germans selling, bartering, and buying. Among other urgent problems, Germany was undergoing a currency crisis. The official exchange rate East to West had been nine or ten to one, but now the (true) rumor was that the Mark would be valued at one to one. For this decision Helmut Kohl received heavy criticism, but it is plausible that he made the proper choice. Briefly, at any rate, many DDR citizens felt suddenly rich, able to carry off TV sets and washing machines at will. No wonder used car lots appeared everywhere in the East.

My next thought after arriving in Berlin was to proceed to the Friedrichstrasse, where I had so often crossed to the other side of the city. The elevated S-Bahn line was blocked, and the underground U-Bahn was only partially in operation. A bus was the single option. On whatever street it was that we took, there was remarkably no wall to be seen – just as it was when I first visited Berlin in 1955. Deposited at its doors, I now entered a Friedrichstrasse station that was another scene of bedlam. Everyone seemed a little dazed, not knowing and hardly believing that one could actually circulate in the halls and passages without encountering control booths, guards, and police dogs. Confusion is hard to grasp and harder to describe, but this was it.

The giddy mood of those first few days was soon dissipated. Only a few months later, early in the following spring, I went on an excursion with my Swiss friends, Hannes Siegrist and Lilli Sprecher, to the Spreewald, a marshy maze of river forks and canals southeast of Berlin. After a touristic boat trip on the waterways, we decided to hike off to a small nearby hamlet. Tramping for half an hour, we came upon an isolated *Gaststätte* on the edge of that village, took a seat on the terrace, and ordered a beer. The proprietor himself came out and proudly served us ... a *Spatenbräu* from Munich.

It had not taken long for the economy to regroup and for West German commercial interests to inundate East Germany, which promptly became a dependent poor cousin of the *Bundesrepublik*. The DDR was no more.

Personally, the timing could not have been better. Having finished the trilogy that had kept me off the streets for more than a decade, I was puzzling over a new project that would extend my research in Franco-German history without repeating it. The solution was a comparative study of national railway systems in the nineteenth century. This challenging endeavor would only be possible, however, if I regained access to those archives in eastern Germany from which I had long been banished. Miraculously, it seemed, once the Wall had fallen, the way was open again.

In the early 1990s, consequently, I returned to Merseburg. In most regards it was the same shabby town as before, but there were some notable changes to be observed. For one, that gigantic statue of Lenin was gone; it now rested on its back, I was told, in an abandoned aircraft hangar. Nor was there any longer a Stasi, something for which all citizens of the ex-DDR – regardless of their station or circumstance – were grateful. A few downtown shops had acquired new facades, rather cheaply painted in gaudy colors, all the better to defy their former patina of dull grey. Also the smokestacks of Beuna and Luna were stilled, allowing my landlady to show me with pride the flowers she was once again able to grow in her garden. The real significance of what was occurring struck me one day when I was driving back to Berlin for the weekend. On that Friday afternoon in 1991, I stopped in Naumburg, a charming small city with a storied past. Around its main square were to be found a house where Martin Luther had once lived, a church where Bach had performed, and an intact ghetto where medieval Jews had been locked in at night by huge gates at either end of a narrow twisting alleyway. Not far away stood the Naumburg cathedral that housed the exquisite statue of Uta, undoubtedly the most beautiful female form in stone since the Venus de Milo. It is also important to know that Naumburg had for decades been one of the principal Soviet military bases in Europe. Standing beside the cathedral, to the right, one could see gates of the main Russian compound that contained virtually half of the Naumburg population. After parking and touring (for the fourth or fifth time) the cathedral, I headed up to the central square, where a huge crowd had assembled. At loss for an explanation, I asked a woman standing nearby the obvious question, to which she replied with a single word: *"Abzug."* That is, the Russian garrison was preparing to leave. Thereupon a small parade, with marching military band, entered the square, and we were treated to brief speeches by the local mayor and the departing Soviet commandant. The band then struck up a slightly off-key rendition of the Russian national anthem (which I had heard all too often on broadcasts of the Olympics) and of *Deutschland über alles*. A muted cheer from the audience ended the ceremony. Leaving this scene, I drove to Berlin as planned, and then turned back toward Merseburg on the following Monday morning. As I approached Naumburg from the north, the opposite lane filled with an endless column of trucks, uniformly draped with canvas so as to hide their contents. What I was witnessing, in its most literal guise possible, was nothing less than the withdrawal of the Soviet army from Germany and, in effect, the end of the Cold War. Presumably those vehicles were on their way northward to the Baltic coast where they would ship out to the Soviet Union. Whatever route they took, they would not return to Naumburg, whose population thereby decreased by half. All of this occurred without a single shot being fired or a life being lost, perhaps the most remarkable event of the twentieth century, one that forever changed the character of Europe.

My next research foray was to Coswig, an undistinguished settlement on the River Elbe between Wittenberg and Dessau, about seventy kilometers south of Berlin. Undistinguished, except for a squat and rather ugly castle in which an archive had been installed to hold papers transferred from Berlin during the war. It had also served for a time, as I learned, as a Nazi prison and more recently as a Stasi internment center. Walking through its windowless corridors was decidedly creepy, an uncomfortable feeling heightened by the fact that I was afforded living quarters in a small building on the castle grounds where, at a safe guess, Nazi and Stasi officers were once resident. It was impossible not to think back to that similar structure I had examined with some emotion while touring Buchenwald. Naturally, on the weekends I took the opportunity to visit Dessau, where the Bauhaus was located in its glory years, and of course Wittenberg, where Luther had famously preached. As a failed Reformation scholar, I was particularly excited to visit Luther's church and to find there an experienced guide, a tiny lady of uncertain age who had often led tours throughout the existence of the DDR. Yet there were disappointments. When we stood at the front portal, she explained that the huge door was actually not the one on which Luther had posted his defiant theses – that had been burned by the French at the time of Louis XIV. And when we climbed the church tower, I remarked brightly that we were treading the same steps that Luther had trod – not so, she apologized, since the original belfry had also been destroyed centuries before. Nor were Luther and Philipp Melanchthon apparently buried in the tombs dedicated to them inside the church. The only genuine piece remaining, it turned out, was the Kaiserstuhl, of which my guide was inordinately proud despite the DDR's efforts to discredit this hideous wooden contraption on which Wilhelm II had place his imperial bottom in the same year before the First World War in which she was born.

Another archive now available to me was the one in Potsdam, easily reached from central Berlin by the S-Bahn connection to the Wannsee. One had only to cross on foot over the Glienecke Bridge, guarded by bored Russian soldiers who took little note of pedestrian traffic. It was still the same old stuffy archive that I had worked in two decades earlier, with a difference that the local Russian commandant was just being moved out of his quarters on the ground floor – a change less striking than all those trucks leaving Naumburg for the Baltic, but no less indicative. It happened that I visited with my daughter Catherine the English teahouse and the castle at Sans Souci on the last Sunday before the departure of the Soviet garrison from Potsdam. Dozens of uniformed Russian soldiers were roaming the grounds, smiling and waving to German civilians and tourists, as if to thank them for their hospitality and to bid them farewell. After that day they were never to be seen there again.

In subsequent years, for reasons to be explained, my investigation of railways also took me back to Dresden, then on to Munich, Stuttgart, Karlsruhe, and finally once more to the military archives in Freiburg. In each of these cities I stayed at least two months combing through every document I could find that remotely had to do with nineteenth-century trains. Especially helpful for my swings into southern Germany was the couple of Josef and Ruth Becker, who lived near Augsburg. Josef is a Bismarck expert – the editor, for example, of a three-volume collection of documents concerning the outbreak of the Franco-German War of 1870 – who had years before invited me to participate at a conference in Augsburg and who now provided me with lodging at his home and useful connections to gain further access and housing in the cities mentioned. Gratitude is also due to my own university in San Diego for financing in 1992 a spectacular tour of tunnels in Switzerland. Inside of tunnels, as I was remarkably quick to grasp, one sees nothing. Besides, a tunnel itself is not extraordinary, since Europeans had long ago figured out how to dig holes. The real engineering feats, I discovered, were the approaches to tunnels, frequently winding and twisting up rather perilous inclines and across soaring bridges. The most important of these, and also the most interesting from an engineering standpoint, was the St.-Gotthard tunnel, constructed in the 1870s, which proved to be the greatest coup of nineteenth-century transportation. It created a great commercial highway between Germany and Italy, and it thereby gave the new Bismarckian Reich a distinct advantage in the competition with a struggling French Third Republic, a topic that merits further consideration below.

Since the conception of my research project was comparative, it was inevitable that my attention would turn back to France, as it did in the mid-1990s. This effort began comfortably enough in Paris, where, besides Montmartre and the Place St.-Sulpice, I found an apartment at the Maison Suger in the Latin Quarter near the Boulevard St.-Germain. This arrangement was facilitated by Patrick Fridenson, formerly a fellow participant in the Bielefeld project, who also managed to sneak me in the side door of the École des Hautes Études en Sciences Sociales on the Bouldvard Raspail to serve during one semester as a visiting lecturer. Since the current focus was on the history of French railway companies and their relations with the central state government, my regular haunt was of course the Archives Nationales, where those papers were located, as well as the musty library of the French national engineering corps of Ponts-et-Chaussées in the Rue des Saints-Pères and the military archives at Vincennes. To enumerate these sites, after citing all those in Germany, is essential in order to explain why my railway study took a full decade to complete before its publication in the year 2000. For this kind of research there is no quick fix.

Along the way, during my excursions to France, I could hardly avoid meeting a host of railway specialists, who tend in France to be much more particularly devoted to that topic than their German counterparts. The Association Historique Internationale des Chemins de Fer, which meets regularly and of which I became a member, has no German equivalent. Three of its fellows stood out. At the old library of Ponts-et-Chaussées I encountered Karen Bowie, daughter of an American diplomat stationed mostly in Italy (where she grew up), who later became a professor at the school of architecture in Versailles. Her marvelous history of Paris railway stations is a classic. She introduced me to the mad genius of French scholarship, Georges Ribeill, whose work on French railway workers, *Les*

Cheminots, was pathbreaking. These two, in turn, passed me on to others, including (as he is affectionately known behind his back) the Pope of railway studies, François Caron, emeritus professor at the Sorbonne and author of the single most influential work on railroads in France, a massive monograph on the Northern Railway Company that has spawned dozens of imitative books and articles while being surpassed by none of them. As the twenty-first century began, Caron was hard at work on an even more massive trilogy that will, when completed, provide the most comprehensive survey of French railway history from the mid-eighteenth century to the present. Despite some fundamental differences with Professor Caron (of which more anon), he and his wife Marie-Thérèse became gracious hosts at their home in Châteney-Malabry and at our mutually favorite Paris bistrot, Le Balzar, in the Rue des Écoles near the Sorbonne. They are perfect examples of a special kind of Gallic *courtoisie* that has no equal elsewhere.

To conclude this account of my travels and travails in quest of a comparative railway history, one episode cannot be omitted. One day in 1995, cavorting as usual in the new modern reading room of the Archives Nationales, I was informed that the documents I had ordered were no longer available because they had been removed from Paris. *Quoi?* Unknown to me, a plan had been long underway to relocate all documentation concerning French private business firms, including the railway companies of the nineteenth century, to the Centre des Archives du Monde du Travail (CAMT) in Roubaix, a desolate former industrial city close to the Belgian border. If I wished to complete my research, already well advanced, I would need to take up residence there. After reconnoitering the place that November, I returned to spend three months in Roubaix in the summer of 1996. To put it kindly, life in that outpost was less than a great pleasure. The archive itself was beyond criticism, splendidly located as it is in an abandoned red-brick textile factory and staffed by a most cordial and helpful crew. But the town is dingy, with an incredibly ugly Hôtel de Ville in the center and with only one restaurant of any note, which incidentally closed for good in mid-summer. With the superannuated textile and nearby mining industries defunct, Roubaix suffers from high unemployment and low self-esteem. Efforts were being made to convert it into a suburb of Lille through construction of a subway line and by opening a branch of the university. Also, an extensive new shopping mall was nearing completion. Yet my Roubaix was bleak, and stifling boredom threatened every afternoon after the closing of the archives. I was rescued from that fate by a television set in my room at what can only be called a flophouse hotel near the archive. My stay there happened to coincide with the O. J. Simpson trial in Los Angeles, daily proceedings of which were carried in the evenings by a Sky News channel from Britain that was blessedly broadcast to northern France. No one has ever followed a soap opera more closely than I did the Simpson trial, evening after evening, glued to my little savior TV set. If I may have acquired some knowledge of French railways that summer, I certainly became an authority on O. J. Simpson.

A reader may justifiably choose to skip over this section. Yet it is fair to ask what conclusions were reached during this long journey through the railway archives and tunnels of Western Europe. The most concise answer to that question was probably offered in the form of a paper delivered at a conference in Lucerne, Switzerland, in November of 2002. One of the precious gifts of an academic career is the opportunity to continue learning throughout a lifetime. And certainly I had gathered a great deal of data about French and German railways from my research in the course of the 1990s. But what did it all add up to? Basically, the problem to solve was simple: how did a single technology, inaugurated in Britain, come to the Continent of Europe in the post-Napoleonic era and develop in a variety of ways during the ensuing century? By 1914 France and Germany possessed the largest and most important railway systems of Europe. How did they compare? More precisely, in what manner were they similar or different? To this day, as everyone knows who rides the rails in those two countries, French trains travel on the left track and German trains roll on the right. Beyond that, what comparative generalizations can be made? My Lucerne paper, based on the already published book, attempted to specify five major similarities and five fundamental differences. Here they may be briefly summarized.

SIMILARITIES:
1. *Tension between center and periphery lasted throughout the century.* There was a persistent struggle between those who favored centralization of railway administration and those who opposed it. By parceling out its territory to various private firms, the French state in effect created a federal railroad system. The number of large independent companies eventually devolved to six, who resisted governmental attempts to impose unified regulations. With no central state as the railway age opened, Germany naturally developed a federal system as well, based mainly on the states of

Prussia, Saxony, Bavaria, Württemberg, and Baden. The new imperial regime after 1870 unsuccessfully sought to impose unified regulations on them.

2. *Efforts to achieve nationalization failed in both cases.* Threatened nationalization of the private railway firms was a constant in France, but only in the case of the financially ailing Western Railway Company did it (in 1909) come to pass. Meanwhile, German unification gave an impetus to plans for nationalization and, in anticipation of it, Bismarck created a *Reichseisenbahnamt.* He thus had a national railroad office but no national system. In short he failed, and he was therefore forced to consolidate the railways of northern Germany under the aegis of Prussia rather than the Reich. This *Verstaatlichung*, let it be emphasized, was not a nationalization but its opposite, because it further strengthened the particularism of the individual German states. This tendency paralleled the survival of the private railway companies in France.

3. *Railways everywhere contributed to the economic growth of Europe.* Counterfactual speculation may well posit that some economic growth would certainly have developed without railways, but the fact remains that they existed and that they spurred the economy of all nations. French railways flattened the price structure of various regions and hastened the distribution of countless goods from steel products to alcoholic beverages. German railways were likewise instrumental in furthering the nation's famous industrial take-off of the late nineteenth century, thereby laying a basis for the economic giant in the center of Europe that emerged in the twentieth.

4. *Regionalism survived in both France and Germany.* The French railway companies fended off centralizing efforts to curb their autonomy in such essential matters as fixing shipment rates, hiring or firing personnel, and controlling the purchase of steam engines (many of them acquired, despite protests from the national state, from Germany). The German experience was not otherwise. Efforts to organize an "operational association" (*Betriebsgemeinschaft*) to implement more unified rates, procedures, and equipment reached no important result before the First World War. Regionalism, not centralism, hence remained predominant.

5. *Railways became the focus of French and German military planning.* After Napoleon Bonaparte, all of his illustrious successors, notably

Séré de Rivières and Joseph Joffre, based their strategy on the swift movement of military convoys by rail. Likewise, successive German preparations for an offense across the Rhine and through the Lowlands, finally incorporated into the Schlieffen Plan, were all dependent on railway transportation.

DIFFERENCES:

1. *The private sector persisted in France but disappeared in Germany.* As noted, the private firms in France continued to manage their own commercial and political affairs with a modicum of state intervention. To the contrary, after Bismarck's failure to nationalize railways of the Reich, the separate German states essentially confiscated the remaining private companies in their respective territories. In this system of *Länderbahnen*, private capital no longer played a paramount role.

2. *Liberalism endured in France but retreated in Germany.* Among other things, Liberalism meant a restriction of governmental interference with private enterprise. In the French case a widely diffused Liberalism was often challenged but not displaced. The traces of this tradition were many: for instance, the absence of a state income tax, the reluctance to adopt (as in Germany) an obligatory vaccination for smallpox, the rejection of a national health insurance plan – and, we may add, the largely ineffectual state control over railroads. German Liberalism, concentrated in a single political party, was a factor in national unification and during the first decade of Bismarck's chancellorship, but his turn to economic protectionism in 1879 signaled an abandonment of his Liberal allies. The resulting decline of the Liberal cause meant that no strong contravening tendency stood against the abolition of private railway enterprise.

3. *The nature of the railway labor force diverged in status.* The unchanged structure of the French railway industry left most *cheminots* as employees of private firms. The companies could hire and fire them at will, determine their hours and wages, or establish benefits, if any – circumstances that promoted the growth of contesting trade unionism and radical syndicalism. Hence the great railway strike of 1910 in France. Germany escaped such an outburst because the railway labor force there was largely in the hire of state governments. Rail workers were therefore, rather like governmental functionaries,

subject to bureaucratic regulation. No major strike troubled German railroads until 1918.

4. *A discrepancy of size developed between the two railway systems.* By century's end German track length was about a third greater than the French, thus accurately mirroring the simultaneous demographic gap: German population surpassed sixty million, whereas France settled below forty million. There were other indicators. Freight shipments from Italy to Germany through the St.-Gotthard tunnel exceeded those to France through the Mt. Cénis tunnel by a ratio of three to one. By 1900 the German coal industry, so vital for railroads, was six times larger than the French. Also, production of steam locomotives in Germany attained a level of at least four times that of French factories. And so forth.

5. *The railway map of Europe dictated contrary military strategies.* After the debacle of 1870 France was in no posture to pose an offensive threat to Germany. Necessarily, then, the reconstruction of railway connections and military fortifications on the French eastern frontier was defensive, and many vulnerable defensive posts opposite the Belgian border were abandoned. In effect, the French high command thereby invited the Germans to adopt an offensive strategy to which they were in any event inclined. The Schlieffen Plan foresaw the extension of new bridges and tracks across the Rhine with long platforms on Germany's western front. The great irony of the First World War, however, was that the actual deployment of rolling stock proved to be of limited importance. After the initial shock, the troops on both sides soon passed from trains to trenches.

Besides Lucerne, these observations were also presented at a conference in Paris, where I took the platform with the Pope himself, François Caron. We could agree, of course, that railroads were a fundamental factor in nineteenth-century Europe and that they well illustrated the character of the two largest continental systems involved. Yet we had differences that I advanced in three criticisms of his work, which were doubtless perceived by many in the audience as an impertinent challenge to papal infallibility by an intrusive foreigner. First, I nonetheless argued, it appeared improbable that a sudden "transformation" of the French railways occurred about 1883, as Caron had claimed (not by accident, since the first volume of his trilogy ends in that year). The notion that private firms were thereafter reduced to the status of a state service does not seem consonant with the archival evidence.

Instead, their autonomy remained largely intact until the outbreak of the First World War. Caron was surely correct, on the other hand, to remark that "a nationalization before the fact" became manifest between 1918 and 1937, when the private railway companies finally expired. Second, I unkindly suggested that Caron needed to spend more time in gorgeous Roubaix, since his archival evidence was disproportionately drawn from the Northern Railway Company, controlled by the Rothschilds, which was not altogether typical of the others. In their separate regions the French companies faced different circumstances. Neither their commercial policies nor financial resources were identical. Such distinctions, like those among the various German states in the nineteenth century, needed to be underscored. Third, the military aspect of the railway age deserves more attention than Caron had devoted to it in his first volume. More extensive research in the military archives in Vincennes would reveal the critical importance of the French army's input for the construction and operation of railroads between 1870 and 1914, all of which was an indispensable factor in the symbiotic relationship of France and Germany. By the way, Professor Caron's defense of his positions (best left to him) was spirited and gave proof certain that his command of French railway history is unmatched. He responded positively to my critical jousting and, as indicated, he did not hesitate to extend a warm friendship.

It seems appropriate to end this chapter by recalling one of its most pleasant moments. Thanks to the generosity of Jim Harrison, an old Harvard classmate of Larry Joseph, I was enabled to spend three months in the autumn of 1996 at the recently founded Centro Studi Ligure at Bogliasco, near Genoa. In fact, we four fellows comprised the first contingent to be sponsored there by the Bogliasco Foundation, and the surroundings in a large villa overlooking the Mediterranean coast could not have been more pleasant. Besides a spacious bedroom and parlor, I was awarded a study on the floor above where I could spread out all my research notes collected in the past years and attempt to make some sense of them. The result was a large chart, with French data recorded on one side and German on the other, which served as the eventual outline for *The Great Train Race: Railways and the Franco-German Rivalry, 1815-1914*. Without question, this was the broadest and most fully realized book of my career, covering as it did both great nations of the European heartland throughout an entire century. When, a few years after the respite at Bogliasco, I attempted to present my findings at Jürgen Kocka's institute of comparative social history in Berlin, I was rather sharply admonished from the audience about the "rigid" structure of my outline (did the critic not realize that I was a Calvinist?). Perhaps, but it seems to me that the comparative historian must shape the evidence to expose actual similarities and differences, and that a symmetry of presentation is essential in order to do so. At the end of the day, to put it plainly, we can only compare what is comparable.

The three other fellows who shared the Bogliasco villa and its delicious dinners were quite remarkable individuals, each in a distinct way. The suave and cosmopolitan John Harbison was a composer of international standing who was finishing the score of his most recent opera, *The Great Gatsby*, which was to have its premier at the next opening of the Metropolitan in New York. One evening he gave the rest of us a sneak preview of his new composition on the piano, so it was no surprise some months later to find a highly favorable review of his work in *The New York Times*. Eleanor Riessa, vivacious and athletic, became my regular tennis foe. She was conducting a study of contemporary theater and, after her tearful farewell from Bogliasco, she returned to New York to become the director of the Yiddish theater there. As for Jenefer Shute, already the author of two novels, she was conceiving a third, about which she remained mum – though I did read the first two with admiration and appropriate compliments. Jenny was probably the smartest person I have ever attempted to keep up with, which also became a physical problem when she and I hiked through the Cinque Terre, five villages located on Italy's rugged eastern coast south of La Spezia, which were formerly accessible only by water and are now served in part by a railway line. At the risk of sounding too gushing, I can say that it was a privilege to spend so many weeks in the company of such a truly outstanding group of personalities.

Any attempt to sum up adequately the decade of the 1990s is bound to fail. The extraordinary change of atmosphere in Europe after the fall of the Berlin Wall in 1989 required that every visitor from abroad had to adapt to a new reality. I can only imagine that an autobiographical account written by an American student arriving for the first time on the Continent after 1990 would necessarily create a record far different from one left by somebody like me whose recollections stretch back into the early 1950s. The intervening four decades had decidedly transformed the face of Europe.

Chapter Nine

SUNSET IN THE ROCKIES

The closer we approach the present day, it is self-evident, the less perspective we have on the past. Although it was crowded with activity, the first decade of the twenty-first century seemed to slip by in a flash. And it is difficult to say what it amounted to, apart from the publication of four books in rapid succession after the appearance of *The Great Train Race* in 2000.

One of the obvious reasons for this heightened pace of productivity was my retirement from the University of California and therewith the relief from teaching duties and academic committees. Caught with the rest of the California system in a budget crisis, UC San Diego offered the inducement of a premature release from the classroom called VERIP (Voluntary Early Retirement Incentive Program), a golden handshake of sorts. After hesitating, I accepted VERIP-3 at the age of sixty-one in 1994. Thereupon I decided to spend my dotage with my family instead of my ex-colleagues, a no-brainer that led me to sell the ocean-view house in Del Mar and move to Boulder, Colorado, to rejoin my two daughters and their families there. Our clan was thus reunited once more, a fitting and rewarding final chapter in my life, without any trying parental chores and yet with the unmitigated joy of four grandchildren.

My new and undoubtedly last home is located on Larkspur Road, north of Boulder, perched on a hillside overlooking the great Midwestern plains. From the exterior deck on a clear day one has the sense of looking off into infinity, not unlike the sensation of peering out over the Pacific Ocean on the coast of California. The difference of course is that behind that hillside stands the majestic range of the Rocky Mountains, with snow-covered peaks above 14,000 feet. Going native, we also purchased a little house in Leadville, an old mining town high in the mountains – thanks to some crazy Italians, with an opera house! – at an altitude of merely 10,000 feet (over 3000 meters). From there we could easily descend in the winter months to ski at Copper Mountain. As there is no tunnel there, I much enjoyed resuming that sport, but I began to notice that my grandchildren, rather than trailing behind their glorious leader, were usually up ahead urging me to hurry up. Meanwhile, the Leadville house was definitely a fixer-upper, requiring new siding, new roofing, and a complete paint job. We chose to paint the exterior a bright red ("hot tamale," to be precise) with white trimming, so that it looked much like many farm houses and barns in New England or Sweden. Every room inside had to be refurbished, and a huge pot-belly stove was installed in the front parlor. To this may be added that summer days up there were cool and refreshing.

But the main arena was back at Larkspur, where I was free to arise every morning and take an early seat at my desk to write. Not that I really had much choice, since my little Scottish terrier Geordie unfailingly awakened me at 7 a.m. and demanded his breakfast. My first task was to finish up the railway research by pulling together notes already gathered concerning various public works projects that had been conceived in the nineteenth century but were not realized at the time, at least not in their original form. This little study of failure, in manuscript called *Paris Dreams*, was translated into French by the very astute Françoise Balogun – who had lived for twenty years with her husband in Nigeria, thus her fluent English – and was published as *Rêves Parisiens* by the press of Ponts-et-Chaussées, an ideal placement for it. The plot, as follows, involved four engineering proposals that met insuperable obstacles preventing their completion.

1. A railway link between Paris and London, conceived (with elaborate drawings to match) either as a tunnel under the English Channel, not unlike the one that came to be a century later, or as a bridge over it that would have been the longest in the world. Apart from the technical difficulties and financial burdens of such construction, the British were not keen to forgo their splendid isolation from the Continent and preferred to maintain their island fortress intact against a possible invasion by European armies.

2. A grand canal from the Atlantic coast to Paris via the valley of the Seine. This scheme was called *"Paris-Port de mer,"* because it would

have permitted the ever larger steam vessels of the late nineteenth century to cruise right up to the capital and dock on the quais of Paris. Thus, presumably, Paris would have become a major hub of international shipping trade like London. Again, the costs and technical complications of such a gigantic undertaking proved to be too fearsome to attract adequate backing.

3. A central railway station in Paris to be located under the Palais Royal, right across the street from the Louvre. As things stood, each of the major private French railway companies had a terminal either north or south of the Seine. Hence the only way to continue a journey through the city, for persons or goods, was to transfer them to other ground transportation. There was no through traffic, no rail link from station to station in Paris when traveling, say, from Le Havre to Marseille. The sticking point for this project was, in a word, congestion. There was simply not enough space at the planned site for a single railway structure to be built that could handle all the competing engines, trains, and tracks that would be necessary for a railway thoroughfare.

4. The Paris metro, which became feasible only after the turn of the century when electricity could be harnessed for the purpose. Original plans foundered on the failure to find an engineering solution for the excess of smoke from hundreds of steam locomotives that continued to ply the French countryside under direction of the private railroad companies. The long tunnels that would be required to cross under the Seine could not be properly ventilated until the invention of sufficiently powerful electric motors. Construction of the Paris *métropolitain* was consequently delayed until 1900 and after.

These essayistic spin-offs from my railway opus were beautifully presented by the press of Ponts-et-Chaussées in a volume published in 2005, for which François Caron expertly added a foreword. Admittedly, as I confessed to him, his introductory three pages better summarized the work than my own concluding chapter.

For reasons impossible to explain, except perhaps through a probing psychiatric examination, I had long avoided dealing at any length with Nazism or European fascism. Maybe it was the clash between my initial childhood impressions, gathered from those awful wartime propaganda films, and the rather uplifting experience in Germany that I later had as an exchange student. At any rate, a bothersome lacuna of my first book on Bavaria was any mention of the fact that Adolf Hitler was present near Munich – in a Rosenheim hospital recovering from gas poisoning – during the time of the 1918-1919 revolution, to which he refers in the pages of *Mein Kampf.* After that study, unlike many of my fellow historians, I gravitated back into the nineteenth century rather than forward to the twentieth. But now the time had come. My approach at the outset was cautiously to tap through familiar terrain by attempting to summarize some of my previous work on the period from 1870 to 1918, and then to extend it to 1940. This brief synthetic account of fewer than a hundred pages, without footnotes, appeared in 2006 under the title of *A Stranger in Paris: Germany's Role in Republican France, 1870-1940.* On the cover, to my surprise (since I had nothing to do with design), was a photograph of Hitler standing on the terrace of the Palais de Chaillot, next to Albert Speer, with the base of the Eiffel Tower in the background. It served me right. Hitler was, after all the prototypical stranger in Paris on that day in June 1940, the only time he ever visited the city. The next logical question was thereby posed: what then? Once German strangers had seized Paris, in other words, what did they do there? The answer eventually came out in the form of a monograph entitled *Nazi Paris: The History of an Occupation, 1940-1944,* published by Berghahn Books of New York and Oxford in 2008.

More dumb luck. The timing of the research for this book proved to be ideal because, for the documentation that I would have to consult about the German Occupation, two large guidebooks had recently appeared in the year 2002: one for the holdings of the Archives Nationales in Paris, and another for the supplementary collection housed at the military archives in Freiburg. What more could a scholar ask for than to return to two familiar sites with a clear agenda of research that allowed for the first time a systematic exploration of the most relevant primary sources? The temptation at long last to take up this aspect of the Second World War was irresistible. It was also a chance to spruce up my forgotten childish memories. Right in the Führer's face.

Looking back over the crowded field of historiography concerning occupied France, it is apparent that we have been involved in an elaborate exercise of putting the cart before the horse. The cart was Vichy, but the horse was the German military administration in Paris that ruled France for four years. Nazi Paris was the main theater; Vichy was a sideshow, and not a very edifying one at that. Yet more than ninety percent of American, British, and French scholarship has been devoted to a study of how the French experienced the war years, rather than how the Germans dominated them. A few German studies have broached the latter subject, but without full access to the requisite documentation. Furthermore, it seemed altogether appropriate for an American historian, in the midst of our military ventures in Iraq and Afghanistan, to inquire about the methods and means of an occupying power. Paris is not Baghdad or Kabul, to be sure, yet it is striking how past events can resonate in our present newspaper headlines – whether it is talk about "terrorists," the use of improvised explosive devices, an outbreak of political assassinations, or well documented incidents of torture. Unavoidably, such matters confronted me with emotional demands that I had not previously experienced. It is one thing to worry about the operation of nineteenth-century railway companies and another to relive the round-up and shipment of Jewish children to Auschwitz.

Trips to Europe after 2000 invariably ended in Paris, Freiburg, or Berlin. There is very little to add to previous remarks about the Paris scene where physical changes have been scarcely perceptible since a major project of cleaning the grimy facades of public edifices and apartment buildings, completed under the presidencies of Charles de Gaulle and Georges Pompidou. One noticeable tendency, which arguably began well over a century ago with Baron Haussmann's reconstruction of the inner city, is the progressive gentrification of Paris. The demography of the French capital is almost the diametric opposite of an American metropolis: the poor have mostly been forced out into the suburbs, the infamous Paris *banlieue*, whereas the center is occupied by the well-to-do. Virtually the only exception left inside the city limits is the ethnically mixed Goutte d'Or, a boisterous section at the bottom of the eastern slope of Montmartre, where in fiction Zola's darling Gervaise once lived. The area is known to me because of a friendship, dating back to distant student days at Sciences Po in the 1950s, with Mimi Barthélémy, a beautiful *Haïtienne* once married to a close acquaintance, now deceased, and more lately to *"mon beau Cubain,"* as she says, in a dwelling on the Rue d'Oran. This is one of the few places where one can still gain an authentic impression of what Paris used to be. For the rest, it is instructive to take the metro out to some end stations on the city's periphery and to observe the desolation of certain Paris suburbs, sites rarely seen by visiting tourists or resident Parisians and underreported on television news broadcasts except for the occasionally recurrent waves of gang warfare, vandalism, and burned automobiles.

As for my scholarly enterprise, some obstacles remained at the Archives Nationales because many documents of the Occupation were still classified. But that barrier is being removed, and in most cases official permission (*dérogation*) to consult these files was finally granted. The technology of the twentieth century has had both good and bad effects on historical research. Good news, for instance, is the introduction of the typewriter, which has made the chore of deciphering documents infinitely more agreeable than the struggle to fathom earlier handwritten manuscripts. Bad news, however, is the invention of the telephone (not to mention e-mails, twitters, and the like), which often leaves communications with hardly a trace and may force the historian to speculate from circumstantial evidence about their content.

Freiburg has been fully restored. All the arcades of the inner city are rebuilt, the public transportation system (as in most German cities) has become a model of regularity and efficiency, and the highly motorized population has obviously begun to take full advantage of the city's favorable location on the edge of the Schwarzwald to fan out on frequent excursions. One of my favorites is a visit to the little fortress town of Breisach on the Rhine. There, in a tiny park next to the village church overlooking the river, is to be found a small plaque, the brief text of which appears in *Nazi Paris*. It reads: "In memory of the Breisach Jews who on 22 October 1940, together with all Jews from Baden, the Palatinate, and the Saarland, were deported to the camp at Gurs in the French Pyrenees." It proves that the Nazis had no clear conception of the Final Solution in the early stages of the war and that they initially thought of France as a potential dumping ground for those considered undesirable in Germany. Later, as my book attempts to portray, they developed other notions. In Freiburg's military archive the documentary material on such matters seemed endless and far more chaotic than the tightly catalogued files of the Archives Nationales in Paris. I was told that the original plan was for Paris to turn over its collection of German documents to Freiburg, but that never happened. As a consequence, the military archivists waited for years to organize their holdings pending a coordination of the two repositories. When that became moot, Freiburg hastily collated its own fragments. All of which could only interest a poor researcher, who must reside and work alternatively in two places and piece the evidence together as well as possible. Still, as mentioned, at least we now have the two indispensable guidebooks.

Three places must be investigated, actually, since Berlin could not be neglected. Both the Auswärtiges Amt and the Bundesarchiv contain extensive relevant collections. Since German reunification, the former has been transferred from Bonn to the new capital city, and the latter has assembled deposits made for safety's sake in outlying locations during the war, meaning that it is no longer necessary for the researcher to put up in Merseburg, Coswig, or Potsdam. While the French have been busy decentralizing the archives, the Germans have consolidated theirs. As for the architectural appearance of Berlin, that remains controversial. Since the Wall disappeared, new buildings have sprouted everywhere, not always to good optic effect. Particularly dubious is the Potsdamer Platz, suddenly once more the city's central square, crowded and overbuilt with faceless facades, like so many brown paper bags turned upside down. But there is an advantage to Berlin. The luxurious West End and Grunewald have been totally repaired, offering their prosperous upper bourgeois populace a level of comfort that is scarcely possible in far denser cities like Paris. On the tree-lined boulevards traffic moves easily even at rush hour, and the immense land surface inside the city allows an admirable dispersal of shopping areas and civic centers. One other comment. When I was first a student in Germany, the only Italian eateries to be found were cheap pizza parlors of doubtful sanitary quality. But by now many of Berlin's finest, cleanest, and most expensive restaurants are Italian. Without doubt, the demand for them has been spurred by Germany's booming tourist industry, which makes it hard to find a single resident who has not lingered on the terrace of some fancy *ristorante* on the Via Veneto.

Did I mention that Berlin also has two more opera houses than Leadville?

The publication of *Nazi Paris* seemed like a proper conclusion to my scholarly career. But I apparently have a weakness for trilogies (counting *A Stranger in Paris* as well) and, besides, there was a further subject that could not be avoided. In the course of my research on the Occupation, I necessarily encountered the singular personality of Ernst Jünger, a writer well known and extremely controversial in Germany, also to some extent in France (where a two-volume edition of his work has recently been released in the prestigious Pléiade series), although he is much less appreciated in the Anglophone world. During the First World War, Jünger was a genuine war hero, wounded at least seven times and awarded the highest distinction in the German imperial army, a medal called *"Pour le mérite."* His memoirs of life and death in the trenches made him a minor celebrity after they were read by the young Adolf Hitler and Joseph Goebbels along with many veterans, and they were translated into English (as *Storm of*

Steel), Spanish, and French. Between the wars Jünger added his voice to those of rabid anti-parliamentary right-wingers who purposefully helped to dig the grave of the Weimar Republic. But he nevertheless resisted overtures from the Nazi Party to join it, and a prospective meeting with Hitler was canceled.

That circumstance, among others, provided the fodder for my portrait of Jünger as a loner who steadfastly maintained his independence and refused to align himself with political movements, notably including Nazism. He was, however, mustered back into the German army two days after the invasion of Poland in 1939 and promoted to the rank of captain. As such he served throughout the German Occupation of Paris with the military administration as a kind of cultural attaché whose main function was to lunch with the likes of Jean Cocteau and Jean Marais. Hence the title of this book, *The Devil's Captain*, shamelessly lifted from Carl Zuckmayer's riveting drama, *Des Teufels General*.

This account of Ernst Jünger's wartime service in Paris is based largely on his journals, now published in full, that were worked up from little notepads regularly carried on his rounds or kept in his room at night. They reveal a self-absorbed elitist intellectual who glides through the city under a carapace of what he liked to describe as *désinvolture*, a sort of elegant superior disinterestedness. He was thus a loner in the German sense of an *Einzelgänger*, literally one who goes his own way with a certain coolness or distance from those about him. I have often had to ask myself if my affinity for this topic – not to be confused with affection for Jünger – does not derive from a similarity of character. That judgment must be left to others. In any event, when the agitation of German resistance leaders in Berlin and Paris erupted in an attempt on Hitler's life in July 1944, Jünger was nowhere to be found. Ever the loner, he refused to join the plot, and he consequently lived on (to the age of nearly 103!) after its failure.

In the midst of reconstructing this story, I entered the main repository containing Jünger's private papers, which are located at the German Literature Archive in Marbach am Neckar, near Stuttgart. During a few months there I had free access to all of Jünger's correspondence, with one exception: the *Briefwechsel* with his Paris mistress Sophie Ravoux. A conspicuous big red dot was pasted on each of those cartons, as I could observe one day while on a tour of the archive's basement shelves. Upon inquiry with the director of the manuscript department (*Handschriftenabteilung*), Dr. Ulrich von Bülow, I was informed that the only possibility to obtain access to those files was to contact Jünger's widow

Liselotte, who was still living at the family estate in Wilflingen. The
chances were minimal, I was cautioned, since previous scholars had tried
and failed. With nothing to lose, I wrote to her in my best German ("*Ich
bitte Sie dringend darum*") and, to everyone's astonishment, she telephoned
a few days later to give her accord. Thereafter I was treated like a prince in
Marbach. What came of this scoop was a lengthy postscript to my book,
which attempts to clarify Jünger's personal life during the Occupation
and after his departure from Paris in August 1944. There is no denying
the elements of a soap opera in this story, a convoluted tale that can best
be illustrated by a single quotation from one of Sophie's letters to Jünger
in March 1948: "What pain for me not to see you any more, not to hear
you, nor to feel, nor to wait for you, nor to live with you and walk at
your side." Yet Jünger remained unmoved and, though he returned to
Paris on several occasions after the war, he apparently did not resume an
intimate relationship with her but instead remarried in Germany. Just
one addendum: following a tip found in the correspondence, I was able
to locate the grave of Sophie and her husband in the Paris cemetery of
Montparnasse. Judging only from their tomb, one would never guess that
Ernst Jünger was the real love of her life, but so he was.

It must appear a bit odd to end the narrative of this chapter standing
beside an abandoned gravesite in a Paris cemetery, but why not? For any
autobiographical account, the author must pick and choose, whereby the
choice is not only what to include but what to omit. It goes without saying
that numerous events of deep personal significance have been left out here:
for instance, the death of my mother at age ninety-seven; fracturing a fibula
in Leadville, not the result of a ski accident but from stupidly stepping into
a hole; my daughter Alex's terrifying automobile accident (from which she
fully recovered); traveling four times to Asia and at last reaching Singapore,
another childhood phantom, only to find it choking with smoke wafting
across from wild fires deliberately set in Sumatra. These and other matters
did not seem to bear on the theme of witnessing postwar Europe. Yet there
are four individuals, for whom no appropriate place was heretofore evident,
that I wish to recall in closing.

One was Gérard Barthélémy, Mimi's first husband, who died early of a
cancer. We met in 1958 at Sciences Po as part of a French student cohort.
Inconveniently, my landlord in the Rue Madame, M. Morin, sold his
apartment and moved away a month before the end of that academic year,
turning me out onto the street. While living in a cramped apartment on

the Right Bank in the Rue de Turbigo, Gérard kindly offered to take me in as a roommate. A lasting friendship ensued that was resumed during my research missions in France at a time when he was living in a village named Verberie near Compiègne, due north of Paris. He and his second wife, with two mature and handsome children, occupied an old mill that actually boasted the name of the Moulin Rouge, though it did not at all resemble its homologue in Paris. Throughout his gathering illness Gérard bore up bravely, taking me repeatedly on long walks that exhausted him but brought us both great satisfaction. He deserves to be remembered.

A second notable person who has ducked in and out of my life is Istvan Deak. He and his wife Gloria (also a gifted author and editor) spent one year during my time at Smith College in Northampton before returning to New York to join the faculty of Columbia University. They soon moved into an apartment on Riverside Drive, where I often visited, for the next forty-some years. Besides being a brilliant historian of Europe, this son of an artillery officer in the Austro-Hungarian army during the First World War is equally well known for perfectly fulfilling that famous phrase from *My Fair Lady*: "oozing charm from every pore...." Naturally he was a smash at Smith. Especially memorable was a meeting with the Deaks in Budapest, where we were received by his sister Eva and her husband Pal Veress, a painter who had participated in the 1956 uprising in Hungary before it was crushed by Soviet tanks. Later Pal visited my wife and me in Paris, for him a welcome interlude of escape from the grip of the Cold War. Several of his marvelous art works now hang in my home, including two evocative water color sketches of Paris streets seen from the window of our apartment.

To meet her casually, you would quickly identify Sylvia Roubaud as the quintessential *parisienne*. Her manners and mannerisms are perfect for the part. Yet her background is far more complicated, as is her character. While her mother was raised in Romania, her father Paul Bénichou was a North African by birth and a professor of French literature by training. An expert on the Enlightenment and a famous literary historian of the nineteenth century, this courtly gentleman became a faculty member at Harvard University (where he was Larry Joseph's mentor, hence this connection). After spending most of her youth in Latin America, Sylvia had a distinguished academic career as a Hispanist and author of a learned book on medieval chivalry, in a word Cervantes. She, in turn, became a professor at the Sorbonne, although she is better known to me as the occupant of a Balzacian apartment in the ninth arrondissement of Paris in which Paul Gauguin was born (yes, there is a plaque outside). Withal, she has managed to remain a modest and charming French lady who just happens to have read everything in every language.

Finally, it would be unconscionable of me not to mention my intrepid publisher Marion Berghahn. A native of Hamburg, she immigrated with her husband Volker (now a leading historian of modern Germany at Columbia) to Britain, where I first met them at Warwick during a lecture tour. Later they pressed on to the United States, first to Brown University in Providence, R. I., then to New York. Since then Marion and I have become business partners in our fashion, as she has – while chief of Berghahn Books on lower Broadway, my *Hausverlag* as she says – accepted no fewer than four of my manuscripts for publication; in fact, six if you count paperback editions. To her, and to the three others presented above, I owe an inestimable debt of gratitude. Fortunate is the one who can count such incomparable persons among his friends.

Chapter Ten

A BALANCE SHEET

What's in a name? Which is to ask: what's in a life? Self-evaluation is always suspect, and besides it is safe to surmise that any readers of the foregoing ruminations – including each of my grandchildren – will form their own opinion of me regardless of which suggestions I offer them to sum up.

My first thought is the inheritance that I received from my parents. Not money, of course, but intangibles far more valuable. My father was not an intellectual man, but he was a careful and thoughtful artisan, sure of his skills and tools. As a boy I often watched him at work, bending over his lathe, painstakingly fitting a joint, or sanding away some imperfection, invisible to others, on a plank of raw lumber. Every object of furniture that he made (of which I retain seven) was literally a masterpiece, with few exceptions wrought from cherry hardwood, stained to a warm red glow, and polished to perfection. Unfortunately, I gained nothing of that talent, but I did absorb by osmosis my father's artisanal attitude. As must be evident from the preceding chapters, I have long carried out my own documentary research, followed along wherever the quest took me, and devoted a multitude of hours to pouring over manuscripts. All scholars, from medieval monks to modern graduate students, would recognize the constraints and rewards of such labor-intensive work, a way of life that came naturally – or, one might say, genetically – to me. It is no accident, given this inbred temperament, that all of my own manuscripts (including this one) have first been written by hand and only then typed or entered into a computer.

My mother was an astonishingly bright and bookish woman. Although she, too, gained no more than a high school education, she read widely in English literature: all of Dickens, for example; and as a veteran Sunday School teacher she was well versed in the King James Bible. She also kept up with contemporary novels. I can recall her passing on to me, then at age about fourteen, one called *The Captain from Castile*, even though she knew that I had little conception of where or what Spain was. Some racier works, like *Forever Amber*, she hid behind the living room sofa where, of course, I easily found them when she was away. Normal as all that sounds, it occurs to me that my mother was always somewhat marginal, coming from an immigrant family and then, as a northerner, living in Kentucky (where schools were still segregated) and later with her widowed sister Catherine Johnson in Alabama, where my late Uncle George had become a professor of engineering at the university in Tuscaloosa. She never spoke with a southern drawl, but crisply and precisely, a manner she bequeathed to her sons. Later in her life, after a broken hip, she agreed to join me in Colorado where she spent her final years as "Granny," the family matriarch. In a sense, I thereby became a single parent again, of my mother rather than my daughters. I visited her virtually every day, which she much anticipated and appreciated, except when my appearance coincided with her favorite quiz program on television, in which case my presence was intensely annoying. Interestingly, in those declining years she never spoke of God or about the expectation of an afterlife, probably because she had managed to outlive her husband by more than thirty years and she had lost any hope to see him again. But once a Calvinist, always a Calvinist. To the end there remained something strict and proper about my mother, character traits that could not fail to seep into her younger son.

More than enough has been said to confirm that this dual heritage of the artisanal and the intellectual was cemented in my personality by that Calvinist strain of character. Such a combination does not guarantee great excellence, and certainly not any genius, but it does provide the basis of a talent for organization, which is the essential quality needed for a wandering scholar whose vocation it is to collect and collate scraps of evidence. To put this notion into a less flattering light, we might conclude that there is something distinctly anal about the Calvinist urge to tidy things up and put everything in its place. At least such a psyche has the virtue of its faults: an emotional stability in the face of disorder and a will to carry on despite a setback or an unforeseen turn of events. My guess is that these personal characteristics were fundamental in the formation of a young man embarking on a career in historical research.

Does that estimate lead to the further conclusion that I was from the beginning or was eventually to become a loner? Again, childhood is relevant insofar as my brother Harry was more than four years older than I and had already left home by the time I reached puberty. Thus I had the feeling of being raised as an only child. My path as a young adult – to Davidson, to Harvard, to Europe – was totally unpredictable and represented an emphatic departure from the pattern of our family. The marriage to a foreigner, the bilingual daughters, the frequent long absences from the homeland, the divorce (completely incomprehensible to my parents) were all somewhat alienating. But a loner I grew to be only in that Germanic sense of an *Einzelgänger*, one who went his own way while yet seeking and enjoying the company of others. Or perhaps in a more subtle French manner that is harder to explain. Most Americans do not realize that the defiant theme song of Frank Sinatra, "My Way," was originally a French ballad entitled *"Comme d'habitude."* The latter has none of the stridency of the American solo version but instead indicates that the singer is rather set in his ways and intends to persist in his usual fashion of self-assertion. That strikes me as close to the mark.

However that may be, the summation is surely beyond reproach that I did stray far from home. My life was not only significantly altered but largely defined by the two student years spent abroad in Germany and France. That experience has not been presented here as if it were unique, startling, or profoundly original. To the contrary, the existence of countless young Americans has been, in much the same vein, deeply affected by pressing beyond the narrow borders set by their birth and venturing into other outlying lands and languages.

Whether this testimony by one witness of postwar Europe has added to an understanding of America's relationship to Germany and France (in the order of my discovery of them) is yet another question best left to others. In my estimation, Konrad Adenauer adopted the sensible and indeed the only feasible course of rejecting neutrality and casting his lot with the West. But implicit in that premise was the acceptance of American dominance. The responsibility of playing the Big Brother was for the USA unavoidable. As a frequent guest in Germany, I could never overlook that political imbalance, even though it mattered little in my personal affairs. All of this seemed an inevitable result of the Second World War. Yet it also appeared provisional, because Germany was certain to recover. Moreover, several unanticipated factors intervened, notably the wars in Vietnam and Iraq, and also meanwhile the end of the Cold War. The outcome has been the restoration of a moral and economic balance between America and Europe. All of us in the twenty-first century will have to become accustomed to this new equilibrium. We can no longer continue to think of America as the eternal righteous victor and Germany as the perpetually defeated and disgraced pariah. That day has long since gone.

As for France, whose troubled connection to Germany has for many years been the primary object of my studies, there has been a bittersweet ambiguity in the development of postwar Europe. As mentioned, François Mitterand was by no means spontaneously enthusiastic about German reunification. No doubt this was due in part to a perception, shared by many of his countrymen, that France and the world-wide importance of the French language were in steep decline, a fact painfully evident in the wake of the war in Algeria. No wonder, then, that the division of Germany was welcome in Paris. But when the events of 1989 broke, France was rebuffed by Russia and out-muscled by the Anglo-Saxons. No less important perhaps, the policy of permanently crippling Germany collapsed from the weight of its own logic. The truth was and remains that, to be prosperous, France needs Germany to be prosperous. To produce French steel, in short, German coal was required. For the German conundrum there was only one solution: Europe. To their credit, the French appear to have embraced that new circumstance even though it means recognizing Germany's superior economic status as the central pivot and powerhouse of the entire Continent. If, for that reason, the French government's commitment to the European Union has been somewhat *malgré lui*, it at least has the consolation that American power is thereby to a considerable extent counterbalanced.

It is no act of false modesty to close with a confession. I can namely find no reason to believe that I am much wiser for my nearly eighty years on this earth. I still cling to the conception that the most individuals can do is struggle to remain upright as their little craft floats through the stream of life. Yet it strikes me that this notion is quite opposite from the one expressed in that famous last sentence of F. Scott Fitzgerald's *The Great Gatsby*: "So we beat on, boats against the current, borne back ceaselessly into the past." Rather, in my view, we are being flushed forward constantly by a mighty and irrepressible current into an unknown future. At most there may be some temporary sense of triumph if we do not capsize along the way – until, ready or not, we are swept out onto a dark and endless sea.

NAME INDEX

Hitler, Adolf, 2-3, 9, 17, 25, 43, 81, 103, 106-107
Hobsbawm, Eric, 80
Hochhut, Rolf, 19
Hoffmann, Ragnhild, 22-23, 30
Hoffmann, Walter, 22-23, 30
Hoffmann Mitchell, Ingrid, 22-23, 29-30, 38, 48-54, 113
Hoffmann Möller, Gudrun, 22-23, 49
Hoffmann Schlegel, Helga, 22-23
Honecker, Erich, 45, 87
Hughes, Charles Evans, 26
Hughes, H. Stuart, 26, 30, 68-69
Hughes, Judith, 68
Hume, David, 5, 37

I

Ivins, Molly, 35

J

Jackson, Gabriel, 68
Jacquot, Christl, 71-72
Jacquot, François, 71-72
Jean-Paul II, 78
Jersch-Wenzel, Stefi, 84
Jochmann, Werner, 41
Joffre, Joseph, 96
Johnson, Catherine, 1, 112
Johnson, George, 2, 112
Johnson, Lyndon B., 39
Jones, Beau, 37
Jones, Peter, 37
Jones, Spike, 3, 19
Joseph, Lawrence A., 33, 42-43, 52-53, 74, 76, 98, 109

Jünger, Ernst, 106-108
Jünger, Liselotte, 107-108
Julius Caesar, 18

K

Kaelble, Hartmut, 80
Kennan, George, 31
Kennedy, John F., 2, 31, 33, 39
Kennedy, Paul, 41
Khrushchev, Nikita, 33
Kiesinger, Kurt-Georg, 39-40
Kissinger, Henry, 31, 36
Kiteley, Jean, 37, 51
Kiteley, Murray, 37, 51
Kleinert-Ludwig, Annemarie, 84-85
Klemperer, Elisabeth Gallaher von, 37, 51
Klemperer, Klemens von, 37, 43, 51
Kocka, Jürgen, 79-83, 98-99
Kocka, Urte, 83
Kohl, Helmut, 87-88
Kolb, Eberhard, 44

L

Lane, Barbara Miller, 31-32
Langer, William L., 26-27, 30
Lenin, Nikolai, 25, 47, 89
Lewy, Guenter, 19-20, 37
Lewy, Ilse, 37
Louis XIV, 90
Louis XVI, 86
Ludwig III (of Bararia), 20, 44
Luft, David, 68-69
Luther, Martin, 89-91

M

McKeown, Thomas, 79
Mann, Arthur, 37
Marais, Jean, 107
Marcuse, Herbert, 69
Marino, John, 68
Martens, Stefan, 38
Marx, Karl, 35-36, 69, 82-83
Melanchthon, Philipp, 91
Mendenhall, Thomas E., 37
Meriggi, Marco, 80
Michelangelo Buonarroti, 19
Mitchell, Alexandra (daughter),
    34, 40, 49-54, 62, 65, 76,
    100, 108, 112-13
Mitchell, Catherine (daughter),
    30, 40, 49-54, 62, 65, 76, 91,
    100, 112-13
Mitchell, George (father), 1-2, 15,
    111-13
Mitchell, Harry P. (brother), 2,
    113
Mitchell, Henry (grandfather), 1-2
Mitchell, Jane (mother), 1-2, 108,
    112-13
Mitterand, François, 40, 74-75,
    87, 114
Möller, Arvid, 50
Monroe, Marilyn, 67
Montesquieu, Charles Louis,
    Baron de, 86
Morin, Joseph, 28, 108
Mosshammer, Alden, 68
Munthe, Axel, 19
Musil, Robert, 68

N

Napoleon III, 81
Neilson, William Allan, 36-37
Nietzsche, Friedrich, 36
Nixon, Julie, 35-36
Nixon, Richard, 31, 35-36

O

Obama, Barack, 75, 78
Oertzen, Peter von, 44
Offner, Elliot, 37, 51
Offner, Rosemary, 37,51

P

Parsons, Talcott, 82
Pius XII, 19-20
Poidevin, Raymond, 42
Poitier, Sidney, 13
Pomeroy, Earl, 66
Pompidou, Georges, 39, 104
Pulchowski, Wally, 34

R

Ranke, Leopold von, 16
Ránki, Györgi, 80
Ravoux, Sophie, 107-108
Reagan, Ronald, 45
Rémond, René, 29
Renouvin, Pierre, 28
Reside, David (grandfather), 1
Ribeill, Georges, 92
Riessa, Eleanor, 99
Ringer, Fritz K., 32

Ringer, Mary, 32
Ringrose, David, 68
Ritter, Gerhard, 11, 16-17, 29, 44, 78
Roosevelt, Franklin D., 2, 9
Rosselini, Roberto, 19
Roubaud, Sylvia, 109-10
Rousseau, Jean-Jacques, 86
Rürup, Reinhard, 44
Ruiz, Ramón, 37, 68

S

Sachsse, Christoph, 79
Saltman, Paul, 66-68
Samuelson, Paul, 32
Satz, Arthur, 21
Schieder, Theodor, 81
Schlesinger, Jr., Arthur, 30
Schmitt, Joseph, 45
Schulz, Werner, 15
Schwabe, Klaus, 17
Sénéchal, Jean, 73
Sénéchal, Marie-Hélène, 72-73
Séré de Rivières, Raymond Adolphe, 96
Shiloh, Tamara, 73-74
Shiloh, Yigal, 73-74
Shute, Jenefer, 99
Siegfried, André, 28
Siegrist, Hannes, 80, 83-84, 88
Simenon, Georges, 77
Simpson, O. J., 94
Sinatra, Frank, 113
Skidmore, Felicity, 32-33
Skidmore, Thomas E., 32-33
Smith, Cecil O., Jr., 28

Speer, Albert, 103
Sprecher, Lilli, 83-84, 88
Spyri, Johanna, 84
Stevenson, Adlai, 31
Stolpe, Monika, 19, 22
Stråth, Bo, 80

T

Tennstedt, Florian, 79
Thälmann, Ernst, 46
Thiers, Adolphe, 42
Thucydides, 30
Tocqueville, Alexis de, 30
Truman, Harry S., 10

U

Ulbricht, Walter, 11, 21-22, 45
Uta von Naumburg, 89

V

Venus de Milo, 89
Veress, Eva, 109
Veress, Pal, 109
Voltaire (François Marie Arouet), 86

W

Wagner, Richard, 17
Walesa, Lech, 87
Weber, Max, 29, 32, 81-82
Wehler, Hans-Ulrich, 80-82
Wehler, Renate, 81
Weiss, Liselotte, 74